BURNING

down

the

DECENTRALIZED WHOLESALE!

Soft Skull titles are available at 55% off for orders of ten books or more. Use our books as fundraising tools for good causes. We want to empower you to spread the word.

Join the Soft Skull Decentralized Wholesale Program.

Send a check for the retail cost of 10 or more books (can be all one title, or a mix), minus 55%, plus $10 shipping, to the publisher at:

Soft Skull Press, Inc.
98 Suffolk #3A
New York, NY 10002
www. softskull.com/wsale
sander@softskull.com

For book trade orders, please contact an exclusive distributor in your area:
Consortium
1045 Westgate Drive Saint Paul, MN 55114-1065 U.S.A.
tel. 651.221.9035
Wakefield Press
17 Rundle St. (PO Box 2266) Kent Town, SA 5071 Australia
tel. 61.8.8362.8800
Turnaround
Unit 3 Olympia Trading Estate, Coburg Rd, London N22 6TZ U.K.
tel. 020.8829.3000

BURNING DOWN THE HOUSE

Selected Poems from the Nuyorican Poets Café's
National Poetry Slam™ Champions

©2000 by the Authors:

Roger Bonair-Agard
Stephen Colman
Guy LeCharles Gonzalez
Alix Olson
Lynne Procope

FOR BOOKING OR FURTHER INFO:
http://www.feedfire.com

OR EMAIL DIRECT AT:
Bonairpoet@aol.com,
Libitlouda@aol.com,
lprocope@lernerny.com,
alixo@mindspring.com,
GLeCharles@aol.com

Cover Art by Ricardo Cortés.
(rmcortes@gis.net) Based in part
on an original photography pub-
lished in *The Source*. Used with
permission.

BURNING DOWN THE HOUSE

*Selected Poems from the
Nuyorican Poets Café's
National Poetry Slam™
Champions*

Roger Bonair-Agard

Stephen Colman

Guy LeCharles Gonzalez

Alix Olson

Lynne Procope

With an Introduction by
Bob Holman
And an Afterword by
Guy LeCharles Gonzalez

INTRODUCTION

by Bob Holman

The image most people have of a Poetry Slam is the Official Word Wrestling Federation version: blood-thirsty word-slingers going one-on-one, each syllable a jab aiming for the judges' emotional jugular, the purpose being to outscore one's poet opponent and emerge victorious. In truth, this is usually what happens. But once a year, a remarkable thing occurs. The gladiator poets mentioned above, who've been busily cutthroating each other all year, suddenly reverse course, bond, rehearse together, write group poems, raise communal funds, and become a "team": it's time for the National Poetry Slam. Outrageous as it might seem, these incorrigible individualists unite, cheer each other on, and travel to the Nationals to try to capture the flag and bring home the bacon ($2000 for First Place, or $500/poet, which usually covers travel costs).

And so it came to pass, in August of 1998, in Austin, Texas, in front of 1,324 screaming poetry aficionados at the sold-out Paramount Theater, the National Poetry Slam Championship was won by Stephen Colman, Guy LeCharles Gonzalez, Alix Olson, and Lynne Procope, coached by Roger Bonair-Agard, the team representing the renowned Nuyorican Poets Cafe in New York City.

Burning Down the House is a record of these poets in the-handy, portable format called "a book." It's what Sander Hicks and Co. do over at Soft Skull—foment anarchic and rev fervor through multi-paged beauties. The 98 Champs fit right into that frame, which is to say, they bust frame.

This book adds fuel to the inferno that is a kind of slam itself, the controversy of text vs. performance poem. Texters maintain that the poem exists solely in print, that what is performed or read aloud is but an interpretation of this text, which is the "real" poem. This gives rise to one of my favorite locutions, "That's not a poem!" which is predicated on the speaker's being able to define what a poem is, much like a slam judge. Once we're in that realm we're talking poetry. What more could one ask?

BonColGonzOlPro are, on the other hand, of the Anti-School School. Performers assert that the poem exists in multiple forms, that the reading of a poem is the thing itself just as the printed text is. If you've learned your poetry from hip hop and slams and television, it's obvious the book does not "contain" the poem — it transmits it. When you read a poem, just as when you read a play, the words begin their work on you. Unlike the dialogue in a play, the words in a poem are not spoken by characters (well, most of the time they're not): the *words* are the characters, and the sounds and rhythms of the words and linebreaks spin them into being(s). Whether read silently to one's self or aloud to others, a poem is made as it connects the consciousnesses of poet and reader/listener. A poem isn't written until it is read, and heard.

This is one way that poetry is making its way back into everyday life: by acknowledging the reader or listener as part of the poem, same as in oral traditions where literature is handed on sans texts. We've always guessed that poetry is useful, somehow — after all it's always been here. But these days, especially in US, poetry is an endangered species. In 2000 you find only occasional reviews of poetry books in the press, and almost never a review of a reading (an essay in last week's *New York Times Book Review* did actually fantasize what might happen if poetry readings did get reviewed, and snidely suggested that the result would be poets going Hollywood. Sheesh!). If you're reading this book, chances are you already know the litany of abuse you accept to be a poet.

Other poets have utilized various strategies and performance techniques to get their words out: usually it's been by calling the work something else, like hiphop (Slick Rick, Speech, Michael Franti) or rock (Ani DiFranco, Patti Smith, Suzanne Vega) or performance (Laurie Anderson, Spalding Gray, Eric Bogosian, Danny Hoch) or comedy (Lenny Bruce, Richard Pryor, Lord Buckley, Firesign Theater, Ernie Kovacs). But what's fresh about BonColGonzOlPro is that there's another poem in their lives and that is the poem that they are living.

> My life is the poem I would have writ
> But I could not both live and utter it

wrote Mr. Thoreau, but *unhunh* reply Lynne, Alix, Guy, Stephen, and Roger. They are living as they utter, and, as the Internet combines text and performance, so their lives , their youthful, joyous, buoyant, grrrlish, poetry-filled existences have earned them a moniker rarely claimed before: they are full-time Poets. They have moved the poem straight into their lives, defining the job as not only writing and performing, but seeing that poetry is available, accessible.

Full-time poets! I mean, they have QUIT THEIR DAYJOBS. No regular jobs teaching poetry or driving cabs. After Roger Bonair-Agard won the Individual National Slam Championship in 1999, he quit his deskjob at Poets & Writers and started sofa-surfing the country (used to be called Barnstorming. Vid. *The Sofa*

Surfing Handbook: a Guide for Modern Nomads by Juliette Torrez (Manic D Press: 1998)), taking advantage of his Moment. Guy established a new slam scene at Bar 13 and retired from the Academy of American Poets. Alix tours relentlessly, radicalizing colleges, clubs, and coffeeshops and is an Artist-In-Residence at local New York City elementary and high schools. Stephen works the performance route and does stints on TV as Prof. Grammar Poet. Lynne performs and organizes the House of Women Reading Series at Bar 13. They are figuring out ways to trade poems for potatoes, how poetry can pay the rent.

Ooo, this is the way I'd like to introduce this book:

> First sweet breaths of New Poets,
> who claim not only the title but the job.

And while I'm at it, I'd add Staceyann Chin to this wave: she who hadn't written a single poem when this crew won their title, now has become one of them, touring, spreading the word.

And as long as I'm on the subject, maybe I should drop the bomb of politics (or is that "balm"?) in here, because that's how BonColGonzOlPro's poems hit. The question of whether a poem can be political is not a question in their work — it's an exclamation. And they drive the poem straight into life, again, via their political activism. They read and march and record for Mumia, against police brutality, for race and gender equality. A poem must not mean but be? BonColGonzOlProChin take up the Be Cause.

But this is after all the Introduction to the Soft Skull multi-poet Slam Champs' *book*, so let's step back from the dynamic and into the text.

How to tell who wrote what is the way into *Burning*, unless you believe that this is a five-headed Cerberus guarding the gate to another world. One of the hidden agendae of poetry slams is to get an audience's ears tuned up and critical. By doing away with the convention of putting their names on the poems they wrote, eyes get tuned up to who's whose, who's what's what. OK OK, I hear Steve Cannon heckling to read the fucking poem so, finally, let me introduce you to:

long-lined polysyllabic, satire to stentorian, ever mellifluous? that'll probably be the work of Roger Bonair-Agard (thunderous applause).[1]

mucho humoroso hip-hop malaprop remixes direct into political vein? tongues trippin with: Donald + Chump, I say toe-may-toe/ 'cause I hate D'amato must be Stephen Colman.[2]

politics and memory in a blender, seamlessly? experimenting with form/inform -ation-ally? webmaster Guy LeCharles Gonzalez.[3]

short-jabby rhymed! Ani[4]-esque dyke! feminist hiphop! ripe type awright! Alix Olson In The (*Burning Down the*) House.

Trinidadian patois? the symphonic reggae conductor of the longest (best?) poem in the book? they call her reluctant? Lynne Procope.[5]

> if Old Lefty Retro is the tip you see,
> let the political surge a sense of possibility.
> watch the iceberg submerge where the doubt
> won't will out, where Will will shout.

figure the jolt of doggerel at the Top contains, as
does most of the language in this book, double
meaning, a Gnostic Ouroboros duplicating DNA
chain, the poem behind the poem rearing its head.
hope this Old School Intro (complete with foot-
notes & John Rodriguez' critical acumen) I've
appended to New School Word Flow is not a textual
intrusion to the oral transcriptions that follow,
that lead.

Will you want to memorize these poems? recite them?
Yes, if your mind can surround, sound, hug, make love,
say words.

These poems be, and mean, and do they ever. These poems
are living things. Read them aloud, a little bit louder.

Bob Holman
New York City
Spring, 2000

1 e.g., "Intrigued by the thought that I could be involved in
the/nurturing of a living thing that didn't jump fences/ and run
all day, I lifted the plant gently to a level sur-/face, as if that by
itself would begin some magic/regrowth." from "metaphor for a
philodendron…" "been bane and darling" from "art & the man"

2 These references are quite New York-centric and time specific:
who will remember conservative US Senator Alfonse D'Amato in
2010? is not the question. The answer is that the Oral Tradition is
engaged with Now, and the Ages will take care of themselves,
because, then will be Now, too. Colman is too busy writing the
poems that are in the world telling it like it is to be concerned with
anthology rites.

3 the "little bit louder" series, which includes slams, features, open
mics and Lynne Procope's House of Women, is held each Monday
at 7 at Bar 13, 35 E. 13 St. in Manhattan. If you don't believe me, log
onto the website: www.geocities.com/loudpoet

4 Gee, Alix, I hope this is ok! I'm a huge fan of Ani Di Franco's, too.
She's a poet in my book. Perhaps it's better: "political dyke"?

5 The amazing "children of a panman an'a maswoman."

FOREWORD

The poetry slams at the Nuyorican Poets Café have long been considered New York City's boot camp for spoken word. Many fledgling writers have cut their teeth before the same boisterous audiences that honed the talents of poets as diverse as Reg E. Gaines, Willie Perdomo, Maggie Estep and Tracie Morris. Subjective to a fault, the poetry slam requires one to come with a healthy combination of content and performance, with just enough arrogance to not always believe the scores, high or low.

It was into this environment that each of us bravely trod, eventually coming together to represent the Cafe at the 1998 National Poetry Slam in Austin, Texas and coming away with their first-ever championship. Whatever our reasons for starting there— freedom of artistic expression, development of poetic, personal, and/or political voice, a cheap place to drink and socialize- we've stayed together beyond it because of a common commitment to the seeking of truth, both in our art and in our lives.

The intensity of the National Poetry Slam was enough to test the patience and dedication of any sane person. All the common ground in the world would have meant nothing if not for the simple fact that we respected and, more importantly, genuinely liked each other. This sense of family and community is the spirit in which Marc Smith originally created the slam.

In some countries, poets face death; here, in the United States, we face apathy. In our celebrity-obsessed and hype-driven pop-culture—where bland, cookie-cutter cliche passes for American beauty—it is difficult for honest art to reach a mass audience. One of the priviliges of winning the 1998 National Poetry Slam has been the opportunity to travel and touch others with work that reflects our personal and political passions. During journeys filled with bad jokes and bad radio tunes, we thrive on the knowledge of our discovery: a community in which we can laugh and rage our way through the contradictory existence that is life in America.

Ultimately, we rely upon our audiences to fuel our energy and optimism. We have not been disappointed. We are especially grateful to Sander Hicks at Soft Skull Press for having the courage to spread our work and, as a result, to be able to share our words with you. Hopefully, they will inspire, inflame, provoke, and ead you to create.

The Authors

Wanna Hear A Poem

I wanna hear a poem
I wanna learn something
I didn't know
I wanna say "YES" at the end
because I'm sick of saying "so?"

I wanna hear a poem
about who you are
and what you think
and why you slam
not a poem about my poem – cause I know who I am.

I wanna hear a
love poem a sad poem an I hate my dad poem
a dream poem an I'm not what I seem poem
an I need poem an I also bleed poem
an I'm alone poem an I can't find my home poem

I just wanna hear a poem!

I wanna hear a poem about revolution,
about fists raised high
and hips twisting in a rumble
like a rumba.
I wanna follow
the footsteps of Ché
and hear the truth
about the day
the CIA killed Lumumba.

I wanna hear a poem about struggle,
so that
when I open my mouth

I can step outside myself.
I wanna listen to no less
than the sound of protest
in the factories
where workers sweat
and make Air Jordans
and Pro Keds.
Because
if you want to take shots at people
target Phil Knight and Bill Gates
contemplate
how they own the products
and they got the goods
how they act like they care
but they're just Robbin' Hoods.

And because every second matters
I wanna hear long poems
and short poems
about time and its limits
because it took less
than three minutes
to attack Abner Louima
to frame Assata Shakur
and destroy Hiroshima
to kill Eleanor Bumpers
and Anthony Baez
to gun down Malcolm
with bullets
they bought from the Feds.

I wanna hear a poem
where ideas
kiss similes so deeply
that
metaphors get jealous,

where the subject matters
so much
that adjectives start holding
pro-noun rallies at city hall.
Because I wanna hear a poem
That attacks the status quo
That attracts the claps
Of the cats with the
Phattest flows
That makes the crowd pass
The hat and pack my
Cap with a stack of dough

I wanna guess
your favorite color
then craft rhyme schemes
out of thin air.
I wanna hear a poem
about
why the statute of limitations for rape
Is only FIVE FUCKING YEARS!!!!!

I wanna hear a poem
I wanna feel a poem
I wanna taste a poem
Give me your spot on the mike
if you wanna waste a poem
I WANNA HEAR A POEM!!!!!

Stephen Colman

elemental woman

I want to be some kind of elemental woman
    the original born before my time
      i have lived this life before;
      on the banks of the orinoco,
            the ganges,
            the nile...

    disbelieving the line,
      because i have struggled
      down freedom's road and
      marched blood red streets in new york city

    un-repressed by religion
      even though i have burned in salem
      and been stoned in jerusalem
      yet still i am faithful, elemental woman.

i need to be an elemental woman
not for this moment but for my life.

i need to stay at home, all alone on saturday nights
    to know the darkness holds no monsters
    beneath my bed or between my sheets
    no club prowlin', no pub trawlin',
I am not lookin' for your love at all
    i   need to stay at home all alone
on saturday nights, touch myself-
in long, slow searching strokes,
to know the wet ain't never been about you – yet

i need to be an elemental woman
    tantric self expression not for you but for my
self.

so i search this world,
for ancient shango peoples
who have lived before me,
who look strangely like me
> follow them to the mystic places
> of dry harsh grass
> wide open wetlands and trees
> heavy with medicinal leaves
> that whisper words to me
> with my ancestors breath.

i go forward in constant quest for my self,
die in the bush country of bahia,

discover how santero drums massage
the heart back to life

i follow my fathers ancestors
in the slave rites of carnevale

feasting my flesh before massa's carnivorous eyes
my silent power in the knowledge that the jesuit
religion will never own my soul

and i will birth beautiful babies
into this world –
> where their color will challenge them with pain,
> before pointing them down pathways
> to their deaths

i want to gather them all to my heart;
assure them that,
> *'everything little thing's gonna be alright'*,
> protect them,

as my greatgrandmother's greatgrandmother
never could protect her babies.

i will be one of those free women
    dancing proud
    wreathed in joy
    clothed in music
like my mother and dawn ann
women of laughter an' loud steelband music
always screaming,
unafraid to be heard

more themselves now than i can ever be

i want to dance beside them
    forever and forever
    singing out halelujahs
    ringing bells of salvation
        from the days of our creation
        to let the music take me back
        to the sun kissing my face
        and the heat cookin' kaiso in my soul
        like callaloo in my pot
i want to be an elemental caribbean woman

    and i will sing a love song –
    i will be that love song.
    resonating so i can hear it sung in my next life!
    a millenium from now to wonder;
    who that woman really was!?!

    - that hint of a melodic memory in the minds of
    men who passed my pride in the street
    and wondered when i learned respect was spelt -self

    that song- of my sisters who stood beside me
    before the mirror, to help me wash off
    another layer of paint and fade cream

sisters who stand with me now as i speak my reality

that i am the womb
before the creation of space

that i have recreated my self
in my own image

to find the spirit of the living goddess is in me
that she is me and always will be
- elemental woman

Lynne Procope

full circle:
upon discovery of some of the mysteries of creation and death

I came gushing into the world
my earth mother's womb pulsating
with rancor, hell & determination
    placenta followed in the bright hope
        of a yellow sun blood
        anger followed that
in the purple coagulations of her joints
        Born into a milieu of combustible volatility
        where hysteria combines with hope
to send one unabashed priceless spear
    sluicing its way
        on an impossible journey

Bold revolution paved my way while
sagittarian pessimism kept me safe
                kept me sane
      but could not all alone
      make me whole

   ...and i have come full circle

through a journey of force-fed re-writes
               rigid discipline
  laughter   violence   sex   crime
      and
        –   peace rallies
    I kept some
   left the rest by the wayside
to come upon a path at once rocky
and as promised as that to emerald city
   ...if we could negotiate the pitfalls

Like Mother,
          I have come full circle
in search of a world she can be proud to leave to her sons
          touting discipline over license
          education over ignorance
          and knowledge over any occupation that steals souls
and curses the lot of the downtrodden
                    Mom said it would come to this –
          -that when all was lost all i'd have is my roots
the memory of my mother's defense
of my wooly hair in afro

                    "he is black fuchrissake!!!"
and my grandmother's high wail of a voice
everyday precisely at six to summon me off the streets
               My brother asked me yesterday
               what he should do with his life
               i advise him with the same bravado
               with which I told him what to do
               to the kid in school who hit him
he was six then
               and his questions were simpler
               i am still making sure he sees my bravado
               but i am a lot less certain now

-     ...and i have come full circle

          back to the arms of those who
     know me most
even when others might love me   as much
          a woman whose lips i once admired
told me it would happen
even as she sat there –
-     pregnant her eighth month with the magic
of Sumaria
     the knowledge of fertility
     sanctioned in her kiss
     and borne in her widening hips –

- you will never abandon her -   she said

Native Fathers
paid homage to animals
worshipped rain
    made themselves whole thru the sun dance
        they knew things came   full circle
            and my grandmother said
            what hasn't met you
            hasn't passed you by
            and what has met you might come again

    -    *full circle*

She survived four strokes
before she told me that last part

    and i fear i may not have prepared
for the comings
and meetings
    and the comings again
        born in tumult
and raised in a halo of fear flight light

                    birth   pain   food   sex   death
                    birth   pain   food   sex   death
                        birth   pain   sex   death

                    birth   pain   death
                        birth   pain
        birth pains
    -    are coming full circle
            and I don't know what has met me

        or what has passed me by

                                    Roger Bonair-Agard

                                                    11

Prodigal Son
a bronx tale...

Returning home to escape my past
I am startled to find that
nothing has changed.

Looking through the innocent eyes of my inner-child
reflecting on long-buried memories
I wipe the melancholy from my cheek.

Sun in my face   exaggerating shadows
nodding along to the incessant bassline of community
as salsa and reggae beats
tumble down from fourth-floor window speakers
battling hip-hop beats throbbing
from the trunks of parked cars
I can see the manhole cover
that doubled as home plate for spring and summer stick-
ball games...

Youthful sweat dripped as small hands clenched
an old broomstick
partially wrapped in sticky, black electric tape.

Waiting for the pitch
my cousin Junior cheers me on from second base
the next manhole cover up the block
and I swing wildly
the smack of ball against stick ringing in my ears
as I put the pink Spalding on the roof of the five-story
building across the street where my best friend lived
until his family moved   crosstown
to Tracy Towers
a world away.

"FOUL!" I yelled
and missed the next pitch
swinging wildly again.

"Strike three!" someone else yelled
and I stomped on the manhole cover
that doubled as the goal line for autumn and winter
games of two-hand touch where the Hail-Mary was the
most popular play and glory lie in having the most
interceptions.

I was always better at catching the passes
not meant for me
and I was never much of a quarterback
except for the time Sean and I got into that fight
and I launched his sneaker clear across the street
because he was bigger than I was
and fought better than I did
and neither of us were allowed to cross the street so
in the end   I won
because he crossed anyway
and his mother beat him for me.

At the memory   a reluctant smile
still bearing the scar from a face-to-face with the man-
hole cover all the way up the block that doubled as a
reminder of how young my father was
when I was growing up
when he had three of us on his ten-speed
flying down the hill around the corner
        him on the seat
        Junior on that cross-piece that dips
            on a girl's bike
            and me   on the handlebars
                navigating
                never seeing that beer can in the street

even after we hit it
flying through the air like some dysfunctional acrobatic
family...

Junior was temporarily blinded in one eye.

My father had amnesia and   sometimes
I suspect that he never fully recovered.

I got thirteen stitches and an everlasting respect for
manhole covers...
not unlike the one I find myself staring at now with an
inexplicable fondness trying to ignore the two fifteen
year-old girls walking by
    baby carriages ahead of them
    futures behind them
    the world resting on their immature shoulders.

    Returning home seeking to relive my past
I am startled to find that nothing has changed
        except for me.

Looking through eyes whose innocence was lost
    long ago
my inner-child reflects on long-buried memories
locking them away for safe-keeping
ignoring the melancholy as it runs down my cheek
    and crashes to the ground below.

Guy LeCharles Gonzalez

Sticks

"Welcome to the stick world," mama whispers
to her newborn baby girl.
She admires the little toes, wriggling
like plump pink ballerinas,
caresses the round belly,
places her palm under the fat behind,
envelops the chunky thighs.
She strokes the tiny flat breasts.
The baby girl sighs
and mama begins her stick world lesson,
hushed and intent:

'We stick baby boys' lips on our nipples-
to relieve them,
stick big boys inside our lips-
to relieve them,
suck until we swallow their stickiness.
We tell our sons only sticks and stones
will break their bones,
then call each other bitch, knowing it sticks
more than hurled knuckles ever could.
We are ignored when our butts stick out,
admired when our chests stick out.
We chant "stick together, stick together," until
size six bitch walks by-
"Sick," we whisper, menacingly, to each other,
"Stick," we think, admiringly, to ourselves.

We smoke cancer sticks, chew on
spearmint sticks, chomp on
carrot sticks, celery sticks.
We crave stick-out collarbones, ribs-
When we cave in, stomachs sticking out,

we stick our fingers down our throats.
Fingernails caked underneath with years of
lipsticks, eyebrow sticks, sticks to cover up
red spots, white spots, black spots.
As we stick to the advice in magazines-
page one: waif, page two: "be you," they croon
page three: "I like a good listener," writes Joe from
Rochester.

So we smile and nod, sticky sweet,
stick jewel after jewel in our ear, so we
swish and sway pleasantly when we turn our heads
to hear what they have to say.
We stick on eyelashes,
lower our eyes in their direction-
suggestive eyes, bedroom eyes, "she wanted it" eyes.
So they stick it in, stick it out-
When we protest,
we are stuck up, a stick in the mud.

We stick our fingers when we sew up
our children's ripped jeans,
our husbands' ripped egos.
We pat stick-it notes on the fridge, reminding
our sons of baseball practice, reminding
our daughters to stick to their diets.
We ooo and aahh over Suzy's stick figure scene,
the first in a series of self-portraits.
And if we are the kind, honey,
who like to stick up into each other,
we stick out— warped Eves.
And even with our combat boots
we crumble like
pick-up sticks sometimes,
away from each other,
and crooked.

Mama wipes her eyes, mascara marring
her Oil of Olay face.
She lifts her daughter's mouth to her nipple,
rubs the padded back,
peers into the clear eyes-
so satisfied, belly full.
"I don't want you sticking flowers
on my grave, baby girl,
mama says,
with the weight of the world
on your stick shoulders.
Crying,
and not ever
knowing why

Alix Olson

metaphor for a philodendron...

When I was 10, we lived in a pink two-story house with
a garage, an avocado tree and a big dog named Bo. Bo
was 4 mths old and looked like most full-grown dogs;
and in a futile attempt to train him, I spent warm sun-
sets trailing breathlessly behind the nervous   clink
clink of his chain against the pavement, after he had
vaulted the fence for his own childish adventures.

me and trim spent our days stoning down the sweet
pungent cashews in the empty lot next door; marveling
at our aim and the fruits' voluptuous sticky ripeness /
... spent our afternoons pretending and half believing
we were men - wondering when the girl across the way /
with the spindly pock-marked legs would show us her -
bush - her gaze always fierce and unaccommodating; her
demeanor more often than not - hostile, we would
return to our homes (buttressing each other with about
12 ins to spare), having judiciously labeled her a tease;
me - to pore quietly over another Hardy Boys Mystery,
Trim - to submit to another one of Mr. Barrington's vio-
lent beatings his brothers (occasionally his mother)
included in a tumult of abuse as his infant sister cried,
my infant brother laughed, and my mother and step-
father provided us all a coquettishly discordant kind of
background music, as they whispered and kissed each
other to sleep.

We would emerge the next day, fresh with hope that our
force ripe manhoods were ready for the excitement of
our other-sex fantasies / full of energy and that swagger
that only pre-teen boys can muster - Trim showing off
his freshly welted legs for the fierce games of soccer we
played barefoot in the street, from little past sun up to

just past sun down ,interrupted only by the occasional-
ly annoying insistence of a passing car, or a silly joke
that made us all convulse in laughter.

I first saw the plant one July / its one full remaining
leaf was bruised and lifeless; the other - a polioed limb
hung by a sliver of a stalk. It was ensconced and left for
dead in an old rusted milk tin under the eave of our even
older pink house; the soil around its shriveled roots a
caste away from dust.

Intrigued by the thought that I could be involved in the
nurturing of a living thing that didn't jump fences and
run all day, I lifted the plant gently to a level surface, as
if that by itself would begin some magic regrowth. I car-
ried a bucket of water to the sorry milk tin with its
dying philodendron (my mother called it) leaves, and
upended the bucket on it almost completing its demise.
Its air pockets bubbled like the lungs of a shot and bleed-
ing man, put my fingers to its muddy, crumbling, earth
to feel its pulse still throb faintly - and massaged the
earth to pack it closer to the reaching trembling roots.
My mother stood over me that time chuckling the cyni-
cism of her adulthood; her hands on her hips, wrists
inward, her own muddy fingers splayed / having broken
for a minute from tending the plants which had already
promised to live; proud of my misguided attempt / to
make Lazarus of a dried and rotting stalk

For two weeks I suffered through the discipline of rising
early to have my life-supported plant catch the nurture
of the morning's first rays,the return to shade by mid-
morning, and a twice-a-day watering and tending of the
flimsy leaves, before I finally saw
           one
               new

shoot.

I kept at this between bike rides down the hill, soccer games that degenerated into fights, foot races from one end of the block to the next, and the crotch grabbing obnoxiousness that lighthoused my impending puberty.

New shoots grew and blossomed, jutted straight out - embarrassingly green and as confident as our boyhood hubris, and longer bolder roots now taxed the side of the milk tin, distending it in their protests for more room.. I lobbied my surprised mother for an actual clay planter - and won; transplanted my against-all-odds creation and watched its stem grow / erection thick and hard, stalks come roaring from its sides and leaves fling themselves laughing over the edge / till like Bo - who still would not respond to commands to heel - I had to tie and carefully train the stalks
to grow strong upright and sturdy.

Almost ten years later, two residences removed from the pink house, Trim's infant sister is playing her own pre-teen games and my infant brother is hanging on my word like gospel - our fathers' long since having proven unreliable. The pock-legged girl from across the way is pregnant - again. The sweet discordance of my parents' whispering is silent now, and in its place is the often humdrum drone of mother's pain, skillfully hidden just below the surface so she can continue her 'strong-black-woman' performance.

I am packing a suitcase to go in search of my fortune / Trim is packing to escape his... and Bo is gone, survived by his springy;   not-so-nomadic son Jah-Jah . It is four clay pots later and the stubborn Philodendron stands in a corner; reserved and strong / seeming to hold the entire living room up on its own.

It is six feet tall.
I am square and strong - "exactly like your father..."
mother would say - and loathe to leave behind a brother
who still thinks me infallible / and I am slow in turning
towards the tarmac, hugging my mother fiercely for dear
life, crying loudly and unashamed, her muddy fingers
transplanting her first born...
                    and still massaging its roots.

Roger Bonair-Agard

releasing the stone to fly

i touch this black man, mistake him for stone
-amplify the timbre of his tears
until it sounds to me as if he is calling out my name
i never know that he is calling out for bone
more solid that this one, for flesh
that is unbroken,
for circles my arms cannot complete.

but i reach for the wide banded breath of his shoulder
pant his name,
incant his coming again like christ,
rest the role of messiah heavy upon his shoulders

his heaving upon me becomes like religion,
my faith in him is all that keeps him whole
-some days.

so i press myself to him and feel the imprint of his scars
mark themselves to each of my ribs
    i give one of them to him
    give him everything i can
    but expect no thing in return

i love a black man, without making myself his shadow,
i make his battles my own,
    declare war on all manner of hard shit
    invite radical thought into my home
    provide safe harbor for his friends
    arm myself
release him to fight my battles
and watch his back,
    i always watch his back.

but i sleep alone
i make space for this man so much like stone in my bed
but sleep as if his leaving me
is not some how an extinction
    i do not dream of him.
but release his hands and remember that we are stone.

stone- porous and accepting,
breathing and eternal.
we have been both foundation and weapon
of choice for the zealots

the engravings on our surface are an anticipation of our
survival
and our substance is hope
our matter is more than divine
we are what god intended with free will

so i choose to love this black man
rewrite struggle in the hard lines on his back
    i choose to love him black

but never in the hope that he will love me back.

Lynne Procope

Repetitive Motions

In the 5th grade
I thought that if I bit my lip until it bled
then clicked my teeth together 5 times
Antoinette Torres would like me.
But then summer started
and a scarred lip covered slightly chipped teeth,
and Antoinette Torres rejected me
at Lisa Skankarella's birthday party.

In the 6th grade
I thought I had the power
to prevent nuclear war—
Thought that if I blinked my eyes
      4 times then 6 times then 4 times again
New Jersey's mango-red sky
      might not remind me of mushrooms so much
and thought that Ronald Reagan would choke
      on his own bullshit
die and let me rest in peace.

In the 7th grade
I thought I saw my hand
      writing on the wall
      drawing blanks
      with an invisible pen.
But then Christmas came
and Santa put coal in my thoughts.
Like chalk dust
faded particles of erased memories
covered my 12 year old body.
I heard the voice of Nostradamus
filtered through late-night television news
broadcasts:

"The world is going to end
Your world is going to end"

I was scared but not impressed,
because you can't predict things
that have already happened,
and worlds end everyday.

In the 8th grade
I listened to emcees roam middle-school hallways
and thought the beat box might help beat back
lip-biting and teeth-clenching.
I fell in love with Alba and Natasha,
and thought that if I touched
Every doorknob and every windowpane
in every room I entered,
I would marry Natasha and Alba
in parallel lives.
I'd have parallel wives.
I see my past through parallel eyes.

In the 9th grade,
paralyzed by the symmetry of my repetitive motions,
I almost failed geometry.
I couldn't draw a straight line
because a sex ed survey
said I had the qualities of a girl.

So I traded my man-hood
for a thinking cap.
I started thinking back.
I went
where the roads cross
where the crows roost.
I went to the crossroads
To the crows roost.

I boosted metaphors
for life from past voices.
I cast choices at glass houses
– just to watch the windows shatter.

I heard the pitter patter
of my Great Great Grandmother
crawl into small tight spaces,
while her parents hid Black Bodies
with traces of white scars.
The light from north stars was not enough,
Not enough light Not enough north Not enough stars
The Underground Railroad ran out of fuel
because it had nothing but Freedom.

If Great Great Grandmothers
and Underground Railroads
can't fuel freedom,
Why should I think I can?
Why should
I think I can/I think I can/I think I can.
Why should I think?
        I can.

America is like a melting pot.
My history is like a melting pot.
And I am sifting through its charred remains
collecting skeletons to hide in my closet:

        My father marched in Selma in '65.
        He never marched again.
        My Grandmother loved Women.
        Her husband loved men.

I am everything my relatives have been
because everything is relative:

I am a Writer and a Revolutionary,
a Nanny and a Cook,
an Artist and an Elevator Operator
I am a Feminist and a Housewife.
I am a Feminist Housewife.
I comb the desert for dinosaur bones.
I am related to history,
we share seamless narratives in common,
we both seem less than we are.
I practice shooting stars

> so I can place them in a shadow box
> with the rest of my ancestors,
> then reflect on the past
> by spitting images of myself into broken mirrors.

I am the cross that I bear. I am the road that I travel.
I am the crossroad
bearing
well-traveled worn maps.
IamwhiteIamBlackIamblueIambruisedIamU.
I came close to truth
once I removed myself from the present,
now I am truth once removed.

I am reflection and repetition,
symmetry and superstition.
I am the square roots of my family tree.
         I am me   I am me
            I am me

Stephen Colman

Fulano

Call me Fulano.

I am a poet
come armed with the gift of fire.

I do not revel in memories of when we were kings
taking pride in conquered lands
my mixed blood on too many different hands
to hate recklessly.

Words of ancestors
with no home to remember
no history to explore.

History is the autobiography of the victor
repeating again and again
as borders cross people
civilizations in ruins
cultures resemble rubik's cubes
several squares missing...
incomplete
incomprehensible
tossed aside like last year's forgotten Christmas gifts
from relatives a thousand miles away
wrong size
wrong color
no receipt
no return.

I look to the future so my children will not die
with the past.

These are the good old days

my father's stories from another time
his father's from another place.

There is no beginning or end
- no rise or fall.
It is now and then and later.
It is other and none of the above.

Our history is a nick in the canon.

There is no Barnes & Noble category for it.
They are not ready.

They are not ready for the barriers to fall
Lucille Clifton on shelves next to Stephen King
across from Aloud and the collected works of Plath and
Whitman
        under a banner
        Native literature

the artist once again known as Prince
plays in the background
the multi-hued masses relax
sip thirty-five cent cups of espresso
laugh at the melted pot
an unidentifiable mass
        humanity...

    Call us Fulano.

We are poetry
the future written on walls of ivory
towers sinking under their own weight
flames shooting from our fingertips
our name written in ash for all to see...

At the base of the tower
standing over the dying embers
the word slammed into irrelevance
I stare out at the crowd—
Romans scream for my blood
dissatisfied with my soul—
the spent match falls from my hand...

To have come so far for this   seems such a waste...

Guy LeCharles Gonzalez

"Fulano is a very old Spanish word for someone of uncertain identity, a so-and-so,...a guy or you-know (as in whatshisname)."

Latinos, Earl Shorris, 1992

33

crossings

        -of the atlantic ocean
        indian ocean
dead seas of unconscious evolution
thru meridians of survival
against traffic at the corner of church and flatbush
        dragging our baggage and burden
        our crucifictions and resurrections
        our praise songs reduced to work songs
        that echo a strange jubilation
        a defiant expectation -

despite the way we are overrun by the
the middle passage
the mason dixon line
    the durability in the slave quarters
    of belmont circular road
    and trenchtown
    their quaint wood work,
    a clinging vine of antiquated architecture.
    lattice works of intricate wood
    winding around shotgun houses,
    like the commonality of scarring on shackled feet
            body to body to body
            nestled so close that tears on your pillow
            soaked into my bed
indistinct lines of blended culture and hybrid tongues
in this delicate death dance of dashiki patterns
between folds of sari skirt

all the lines,
break –

these ancestors echoed
dense rhythms

their the conviction
of our footsteps

they sounded the caveat call of our coming

- if a cadence and gychee wisdoms
of patience and time;
of durability and passing
shango power baptized believers in
divination across bodies of water
that hold our stories

despite crossing great divides
      small, island sounds
      mixed into big city beats
      and all accents sound like mother continent
roll wide as pacific waves, deep as ska beats and broad

      as broadway
      42nd street
      grand concourse
      fulton street
this fostered promise land
is not mecca, el dorado, serengeti;
is not home.
is a tight construct of dream and nightmare
of calculation and urgency
it is callow and ephemeral;
only a flirtation with humanity
with is unsupported truths,
its well imagined reality.

we have crossed oceans and continents of earth
to find ourselves lost on these littered shores
whose faults have sifted countless times
beneath our feet

- and crossed sound barriers
sucking creole tongues into our mouths

we have crossed thresholds of pain
shrugging the shrouds of scar tissue from our backs,

crossed the divides of loss
to commune with loved ones
come to know them as ancestors
understood ourselves as one.

we have crossed blood-inked pages
worded with stolen histories,
recaptured joy and taught each other truth.

we crossed narrow broken roads
to know our possibility
to survive the horror of this reality
and now we are loathe to turn our backs
to retrace our crossings,
to admit any single defeat.

these journeys have readied us,
these middle passages return to us
the jubilation
of survival songs.

Lynne Procope

how do we spell freedom
– the weusi alphabeti method

I

In 1970 I learned my alphabet
 for the very first time
-     knew it by heart in 1971
A is for Africa
B is for Black
C is for culture and that's where it's at
my mother taught me that from the Weusi Alphabeti
     at a time when A was for apples in a country that
     grew mangoes
     and X was for xylophone when I was learning
     how to play the steelpan
black wasn't popular
or even accepted then
     but I wore dashikis sent me from nigeria
          super-fly suits; sky blue with the elbow patches
sent me from america
and sandals made by original rastafari before weed &
revolution needed fertilizer to grow
          my mother rocked bright saffron saris
we were phat 20 years too early and a thousand miles
removed
my mother preached hard work
knowledge and how not to take shit
D is for Defense
E is for Economics

II

I wrote my first protest letter at the age of 3
to my grandfather
for calling me in out the front yard
spelling fuck you with an
    f - o - r - k - U
put it under his pillow in the hope
        it would blow up and burn his ear off at night
    wanted to get started on this revolution thing
F is for Freedom

III

G is for Guns – we gotta get some
  Weusi said

evolved into 1979 and a revolution with a changing face
  * bang bang boogie to the boogie
  say up jump the boogie – let's rock – yuh don't stop
black folk and brand names became entwined
we re-invented dance and made wheels roll
with a limp
Cuba had just told America he was Africa in Angola
K is for Kings
L is for Land – we gotta get it back

  so we lost Jamaica to the IMF
  Grenada to the marines
  and Panama to Nancy Reagan
jherri curls became high top fades, became gumbies,
became caesars
as Michael Jackson moonwalked his way into a lighter
shade of pale
  my mother sent me to america – she said
"Go fix that!"

IV
K is for Kidnap
S is for Slavery   - Weusi explained

cool became   buttah became   phat
     we lost our focus and our way
just at about the time
black folk outside the nation
discovered the dangers of pork
     so fat backs became phat blacks
     pigtails became dredlocks
     and fades faded to bald
as Michael Jordan discovered the magic of a fadeaway
jumper
     and endorsements

X is for the niggah who's blind deaf and dumb
     X him out - Weusi said
my mother told me I should re-write that
that X is for the nigga who needs to be re-educated
that a corporate job does not spell freedom
marry white don't mean racist flight
a democratic vote is not a revolutionary act
          and as long as there's a sweatshop in Jakarta
there is no difference
between Patrick Ewing and O J Simpson

V

God gave Noah the rainbow sign
-   said no more water; the fire next time
J is for James Baldwin – next time is now

H is for Huey
N is for Nat Turner
T is for Tubman
M is for Malcolm, Mandela, Marley & Martin got shot
two weeks after he told black folk to boycott Coca-Cola
Jesse Jackson still scared of niggaz with a purpose

- and someone must learn to read the signs with me.

Roger Bonair-Agard

Framework in it

I'm fantastic
My words are like elastic
I wrap verbs abound nouns
And stretch sentences in to plastic
It's like em to the phatic
Acro to the batic
Like friction leads to heat
Bad diction causes static
I break my rhymes into fractions and to particles
I use the present tense
Then switch the verse to past participle
My articles precede my adjectives i had to give a vowel
away
Now I don't have none left
I'm at a loss for words
I must report this theft
'cause I'm not hardly
even partly
interested in your grammar
pull the rug
release the plug
and snatch the film from out the camera
I go through phases
I write my lines in stages
I put tropes within quotes
And bust narratives out of cages
My pages place parts of my poems
Within parameters
My pencil's like a stencil
As I sketch out these diameters
    Because
    I work my frame
    And my frame/works me

Just like I shake my hips
And my hips shake me
Check out the space that I create
Between each verse
And in my consonants
I purse my lips
To demonstrate my verbal competence
I set break-beats
Like bed sheets that are mad tight
My lyrics leak out
From the eraser to the graphite
I crack through ceilings
I'm a comma chameleon
Periods pace my pauses
Semi-colons trace my feelings
I cross my eyes
Then I pot my teas
It's the keys my fingers type
That unlock apocryphies
I possess apostrophes
Obsess on stormy c's
I got bit in the but(t) by a swarm of killer b's
I freeze in rough drafts
Then indent my paragraphs
Each clause is like a gauze
To protect from verbal gaffs
I make alpha-bets
On exclamation point spreads
I pull book covers back to unwrap my mast head
My nose grows
When I impose
An "I suppose I could be right?"
My lyrics bloom
When I expose them to the light
I beat wack poems
Into phat tomes

Then stack cracked clones
Into concrete
I riddle holes in syllables
Then think Up thoughts
On the downbeat
Because the prose that I compose
Controls my foes and flows alike
I strike a pose
When I rock up on the mike

Stephen Colman

handmade memories

there is something
about the hand
        sh – sh – sh – shaving
of a block of ice
on a day so hot
the concrete ripples

the sticky sweetness of
        mango – coco – piña
poured from hand-labeled
bottles through plastic
spouts over chips
of ice packed tight
into thin paper cones

the sweaty trickle
    between your fingers
        around your thumb
           across your wrist
               tongue flicking fast
before it falls to the ground

there is something there
that reminds me of home

Guy LeCharles Gonzalez

sinking suns and city wishes

Here where the land is hard
  sunsets do not bleed soft and blithely across a sloping
sky
 do not lend canvas-like swatches of effect
for the cheering of onlookers

Here where the land is hard
 the bastard sun sinks like a stone in a pond
only staring one-eyed and harsh yellow
into its temporary death

We wait for the sun to perform
  demand jabs of color
and cloud stained stylishness to end our days
but strawberry and lettuce and grapes and artichoke
grow here under the duress of slave wages
– campesinos live and die
with little ceremony and no fanfare
we trade their lives away cheap   for a little
fresh fruit & greens everyday;   and then ask for enter-
tainment

Our star; our diva sun pouts
  refuses to reward this land
with his carnival flair – his costumed dance
he saves; waits in the wings for music
worthy of his more colorful plumage

In the meantime, he will allow only
  the danse macabre - a monster dance in portrayal
cyclop-guarding a land he loves and mourns-
-so he can only haul in the reins of his heat
  and hope he hears in the ramshackle homes

of the campesinos; a mariachi tonight
any song which might tell
   that one more of his children has made it through
the day – that one more of his children will survive
to pay him proper tribute

Imagine our gall – keeping vigil
  across the plains of this burnt harsh land
disappointed that nature might deny us
pose and flex   here where the land lies hard
and we squeeze a little more worth out of it every day
crisscrossing sprinklers magically in the twilight
      in search of a softer ground   an easier yield
a more lush harvest

Here where the land is hard – we travel from
amongst our skyscraped homes in search of sunsets
and the nights ambient lights and return disgusted
and forlorn; curse the heat or the cold
  complain on our own rough lots in life
roughly break off another strawberry bulb
   and bed down for the night

Roger Bonair-Agard

New York New York

New York New York
big city of dreams—
Where investment bankers feed us bull
markets
and greedy guys named Merrill
lynch low-income workers
    leaving them in stocks in bonds.

Where suburban tourists go
Christmas sweatshopping at Macy's
and Donald Chump changes
landscapes to skyscrapes
uses his 9 wives
then counts his lucky tax breaks.

    And it's not safe to cross the street
    because you might get a ticket for jaywalking
    and even cooks get arrested for panhandling.

Where it's not prudential
to sell a piece of the rock
unless you're a cop.
I've got the NYPD Blues.
I can't sleep
from all the police protection racket
outside my window
because Wall Street brokers
aren't the only tough guys in blue suits
who trade securities for profit –

In the city that never sweeps
public services get trashed.
The Bored with Education

sacrifices its pupils for private eyes.
Hunger cramps replace food stamps.
Crime pays. Jail sells.
Politicians can't create jobs,
So they hide the unemployed
in the basement
or the Attica
and Mama I Wanna Sing Sing!
and dance!
but I can't
because I don't have permit.

New York New York
big city of dreams—
Where CEO's try and look real cute
in their sear Sucker suits
but they sell their souls for the cash and the loot.
Like Giuliani
The Lying King
who lives in Disgracie Mansion
and plays his Annette Funi-Cello
for Michael Eisner.
I wanna put Disney on Ice,
because they replaced triple x's
with triple lutz's,
pushing their own brand of kiddie porn
and pimping Pocahontas on 42nd street.

New York New York
big city of dreams—
Where downsizing
plus workfare
divided by color class and gender
equals the Dow Jones Industrial Average,
there is no remainder.
And you don't need a

Sony theater to see
Dead Men Walking
just go to city hall,
where we need a Truth Messenger,
not a Ruth Messinger.
I say toe-may-toe
'cause I hate D'amato,
and when I win the lotto
I'll call a citywide strike,
because if Giuliani has his way,
"Everything is gonna' be all white."

New York New York
big city of dreams.

Stephen Colman

America's on Sale!

ATTENTION SHOPPERS!!!
attention 9 to 5 folk, cell-phone masses,
the "up and coming" classes,
attention sports-utility,
plastic-surgery suburbanites,
viagra-popping, gucci-shopping urbanites
attention george-clooney loonies,
promise-keeper sheep,
stockbroker sleep-walkers,
big investment talkers,
ricki lake watchers,
attention walmart congregation,
shop til you drop generation,
ATTENTION NATION!
AMERICA'S ON SALE!

we've unstocked the welfare pantry
to restock the wall street gentry
it's economically elementary,
because values don't pay,
yes, american dreams are on permanent layaway,
(there was limited availability anyway)
so the statue's of liberty's being dismantled,
$10 a piece to sit on your mantle or hang on your wall
by the small somalian child
you bought from sally struthers
sisters and brothers, it's now or never,
these deals won't last forever-
AMERICA'S ON SALE!
(restrictions may apply if you're black, gay or female).

and shoppers,
global perspective is ninety-ninety percent off

cause most of the world don't count to us
our ethic inventory's low
cause moral business has been slow,
yes, the values-company is moving to mexico—
and ALL ETHICS MUST GO!

it's a remote control america that's on sale
cause standing up for justice can't compare
to clicking through it from a lazy chair:
Answer: jerry, montel, oprah
Question: folks who really care...for $1,000,000,000!

in this new mcveggie burger world order
where national health care is
one-hundred percent off !!
and medicare's in the 50% bin,
so you can buy...
half an operation
when AMERICA'S ON SALE!
and there's a close-out bid to determine
which religion will win
all the neon flashing signs of sin
the christian coalition is bidding high-
shoppers, you ask WHY!
who needs a higher power when
you've got the purchasing power to corner and market
one human mold.
that's right- Real Family Values are being UNDERSOLD!!

and it's open hunting season for the NRA!
There's a special oozie discount— only today!
Gun control?? We say—
black bear, black man, blow em both away!
and Guiliani welfare mamas
are on the auction block again,
we're closing out this country the way we began.

so step up for our fastest selling commodity
no waiting lines for HIV,
condoms and needle-exchange are a hard to sell thing
(to the right wing)
so if you're a druggie or a fag-
Rent-to-Own your own body bag NOW!
WHILE AMERICA'S ON SALE!

we're selling fast to the AT&T CEO,
he's stealing all utilities,
he doesn't pass go,
and collects $1,000,000 anyway,
he's the monopoly winner
because he bought the whole board
and we bought the whole game
now no price is the same!
cause inflation's up on the CEO ego
and power's deflated as far as you go:

cause Nike bought the revolution
and lawschools bought the constitution
tommy hilfiger bought the red, white, and blue,
a flag shirt for fifty dollars,
the one being burned is you!
marlboro bought what it means to be a man
lexus equals power- get it while you can
maybelline bought beauty,
new york's buying rudy
mastercard gold bought the national soul
Broadway bought talent and called it CATS!
the republicans bought out the democrats
they liquidated all asses in a fat white donkey sale-
now it's buy one shmuck, get one shmuck free
in the capitalist party!
and there's nothing left to get in the way
of a full blue-light blow-out

of the U.S. of A!

there's a no-nothing back guarantee,
a zero-year warranty,
when you buy this land of the free-tos, ruffles, lays..
this home of the braves, the chiefs, the reds, the slaves!
so call 1-800- i- don't- care- about- shit
or www . FUCK ALL OF IT.
to receive your credit for the fate of our nation-
(Call now! Interest is at an all-time low)

so with these sales-pitching verses
i should win for customer service
i'm like CRAZY EDDIE—
i'm GOING INSANE IN AMERICA!!
where the almighty dollars sparkle and shine,
this Star Bucks Land that's yours and mine.
but america's selling fast shoppers.
BUY IT ALL WHILE YOU CAN!
cause america's been downsized, citizens.
and you're all fired.

Alix Olson

Head Trip

I planned an armed rebellion
from bed last night
but the F.B.I. tapped my dreams
They heard Wall Street scream
took notes
when I stole the crack
from the liberty bell
and used it to free Mumia from his cell.
They followed my sentences
when I said
"chains link slaves and fences,"
like the past leaks tenses.
Before the past tense there was the pre tense.
My dreams sensed past tension.
I passed tension
on the way to revelation.

I turned Left.
Nothing was Right.
I got caught under cover of night.
And the bright light
in my brain came
from an interrogation lamp
        stamped "govt. property."
They rode my mind's waves for snapshots
of C.I.A. crackplots,
while crackpots planned
jackpots in foreign lands
from the sands of Iraq
to the shores of Nicaragua,
for agua and oil
gold zinc and soil
paybacks to fatcats by gatt-pacts

for economic heirlooms
while cops jacked Black Kids in backrooms...

I thought uprising
but Dionne Warwick tipped off the D.E.A..
They probed my nose
for the welfare lines I sniffed
found factory lines instead.
Because only chimney's smoke in my dreams.
Only newt gingriches get smoked in my dreams.

I planned an armed rebellion from bed
        because I'm tired
of counter revolutions —
        store-bought brand-name resistance.
Cash cannot register change,
only people can.
Because revolutions
depend upon the gravity of the polar axes
we have to grind.
It's the never mind
that can't see the future.

So now my dreams practice killing
random acts of senseless silence
because quiet violence
never met an empty space it did not like.
And in my dreams I wake up
and greet the government agents
posted in my head
with a smile.
I rise up.
I keep on rising.
keep on rising
        to the bottom,
because the top holds things down.

And the only sound
You'll hear from my sleep,
the only movement
I make in my sleep
is Revolutions
Turning   Turning
            Turning.

Stephen Colman

Untitled

we be pretenders,
pretenders to the position of prophet.
we don the mask of poet
late at night and between the smokes
and the lyrical jokes - we slam
up on that mic.
then just for fun
we dare to dun
the rubric of your revolution.
We stray to play the word
for audiences of the herd,
prostitute the power of our pens
- in whoring for those tens
    and we forget
    that this shit goes beyond gil scott
    goes beyond the grand slam finals plot
    this goes beyond these half-assed rhymes,
    we done forgot

this art is an echo, it is a word, it is a pain,
a tear in the heart of the people
who do not have the time
to spend etching catchy lines,
    when you earn under $5.25 an hour
    and double up on jobs
    just to buy milk or fruit or flour

it is the lost voice of the loisaida,
plymouth rock, tienamen square, fulton street
and death row
because we will never know
what we have lost
if our poets don't tell us about

the linear nature of our oppressors
if our poets don't re-write the riot act
and the miranda advisement
    -we have no right & no reason to remain silent!
    we must rage a joyful, powerful, angry noise
        if we remain silent
        they believe that they have won
    anything we say must speak to truth
        - the innocents are listening
    can and will must be our watchwords
    we must watch words before they are held against us
        or taken away
    poet and humanity must hold each other
    and remember

        that our – revolution has not been televised
        it must not be demonized
        it must not been marginalized
    and it never basketball!

this art is a coming home,
a reclaiming of boriqua land ,
a relearning the ghost dance of black elk
because the language and rhythms of our ancestors
died a little bit,
        every day they were silenced.

this is the trial by fire of militant ire
the art of spoken word-
goes beyond conjugation of the verb

it is the invocation to act

the evolution of thought

and the way we know that we are not alone,

poet-   did you read fanon, shakur
or maybe one of the barakas?
did you ever cry when willie told how petey died?
did fela ever make you stamp
or rudder make you shine?
or marley make you lift you head to jah on high?
did you read? have you listened?

Do you know the definition
of your revolution...
or are you just pretendin' when you step up to the mic?

1 - 2, 1 - 2, - ...this thing is on!

Lynne Procope

33-1/3 Revolutions Per Minute
a love poem for Friday night revolutionaries...

The revolution has been—
> the revolution has been—
>> the revolution is in danger
>> of becoming a has-been.

Hip-hop has failed its mission
straying from its destiny as the poetry of the people
rock & roll's sequel in its soulless quest for mass appeal.

Well I *Been around the world and*   *I*   *I*   *I*

I've seen history repeated
> too many times by
> too many people
> that should know better.

Slavery was replaced by the music industry
house niggers go to the highest bidders
keeping the revolution underground
>> undermanned
>> undermined

so I'm tired of waiting for poets to open their eyes
and reject the status quo.

Complacency is an angel of light
everything's not all right
'cause the CIA could be tapping my phone.

One false move and my death becomes a mystery the Las
Vegas police won't bother to solve
> and though I'm ready to die

I've realized that the revolution
does not need another martyr.

Biggie failed to see this reality
    succumbing to self-prophecy
        selling his soul
        thinking he'd get money
        from his playa-presidency to buy it back.

All caught up in stereotypical fantasies
        ...that gangsta mentality
        that's killing us softly
as the DEATH of the revolution is televised nightly
the number-one rated show on MTV
starring Puff Daddy and Jay-Z
    with thick bass licks from '80's pop hits
    supporting stupid-ass lyrics
    spurting from the lips of Versace-branded slaves
turning my stomach late at night when I find myself
        dancing to it

    ...lost in that bass line
    reality shrouded
    my mind clouded

my hands where my eyes   CAN'T see
forgetting how it used to be

...it's all about the Benjamins now
as hip-hop heads become wannabe's
Gil-Scott Heron collects his royalties
and the revolution is a commercial property
    pimped by Sprite   and the NBA...

            ideals are nothing
            image is everything

Jordan got one last ring and
Mumia's plight is a hollow slogan
           to hook a poem on

So I'm tired of seeing the revolution compromised
by wannabe rap stars disguised as slam poets
pandering to the crowd
           telling them what they want to hear
           instead of what they need to hear.

Thoughtless words like mad-cow disease
wiping out an entire generation
so I poke you in your third eye to clear your vision
           realize that you're the problem
           not the solution.

You're not a poet
you just slam a lot
      cram a lot of senseless rhyming
      soulless pantomiming
      saying shit like   *Tommy Kills-niggers*
'cause it's always fashionable to lay blame elsewhere
especially if gets a laugh and a couple of extra points.

Store-bought politics from brain-washed hypocrites
sweet-nothings disguised as calls for revolution
           designed to win the Slam
           disguising true intentions...

      grab a blunt and a forty
and that bleach-blonde shorty you dissed from stage
           patronizing the black woman's rage
           acting lactose intolerant
           knowing damn well that   you got milk.

Sometimes
the thieves in the temple are the priests themselves
and despite my own glass house
I dare to throw stones
'cause it takes a clean break   to heal right
and I can't let the revolution go on
        without you...

Guy LeCharles Gonzalez

My Daughter

For my amazon babes, male, female and in-between

I'll teach my daughter to bang on
anything that makes a beat
She'll shake-a-boom, she'll quake a room
She'll paint her cheeks warrior-style, then smile
Beguile you, turn you inside out
til your guts plead guilty
She'll be built like a truck, built to work you down
As she works herself up
She'll make holes in the street
in her ten inch spike heels,
In combat boots, stilts, on roller wheels,
She'll stroll through Male Pride
Amazon Babes at her side.
She'll relinquish White Privilege
Observe, be wise, she'll compromise
When the fire is stoked by some other woman's desire
But she'll never leave the flame.
All the same, she'll crave what makes her burn
She'll learn her Cunt's good name
The layered liquid lips and little hot tip
No more of this cryptic shit-
This Vagina will be known.
She'll poke in all the wrong places
she'll park in all the wrong spaces,
make faces at police cars,
wind up behind bars,
bust out big before serving her time,
fingernails full of this grime we call
Reality,
She'll dig her way through.
She'll pick her nose when she has to,
She'll scratch her ass,

She'll be a crass medusa child
A wild healthy field
She'll live in all fonts and all sizes:
Curly q's, caps, italics, and bold
She'll fold airplanes out of shredded
Cosmos and Mademoiselles,
Then pilot them to Never-Say-Never Land
Where Peter Pan's gay and Wendy's
Ok with it.
She'll wear thick braids, she'll shave her head,
She'll eat thick breads, she'll let her breasts flop,
She'll mop the floor like Cinderella,
then with rebellion-prowess,
She'll unionize daughters for a higher allowance.
She'll be male and female and
In-between
She'll preen, then crack her mirror, crack a beer
And watch Love Connection.
She'll go for days without taking a shower
Just to feel unchained Ivory-slave power.
She'll want more than what she's 'entitled to'
She'll watch through Nike commercials and she'll
Just Un-Do It
Ask who's making that shit, who's breaking their backs
Keeping her breaking that
Glass Ceiling
She'll do all of this.

And she'll do none of this.

And it's funny how we hide behind these daughters,
Hide ahead of our own Herstories
Scared of ourselves, scared of the world
Scared of someone who made us
One way
Or another

Well, this time around
I'll be bound to my own
Mind Womb
In my own birthing room,
I'll squeeze out
Squeeze out
Each crimson thick belief
Then eat each pungent, sweet placenta
And relieved,
I will tear up this country's
"Welcome to the World" certificate,
tear off my father's father's father's father's
name,
I'll legitimate my own entrance into a
Thinking Existence
I will birth myself towards
Resistance.
But no frantic tick-tock of this Biological Clock.
On my own time, Foremothers at my sides,
Sisters as midwives,
I'll cut my cord, head for that War
I will mother myself
into my own grown daughter
And I will call myself
A Home-Grown
Wommin.

Alix Olson

hard work love and winter blues

He saunters broad-shouldered and bad-john sure
 into the bar notes the contrasted heat
long ropes of hair noosing one another unruly
    he will sit a minute here
    orders bourbon neat

        Just outside the Loop
        in a Chicago West-Side bar
        no-one knows how cold it is
or that it's Christmas - the savior is come
        that spring is a stretch away

They have chosen to forget such things
 twinkling lights cannot fool them
 the world is no brighter than a stranger's absent smile
He buys a petit-quart as is his Caribbean way
 offers the change on the $20
 back to the buxom wide-hipped waitress
  moving easily behind the bar
black overalls over a slinky red short bodice
revealing a hint of black bare belly
spreading like slow nightfall toward her hips

He
    smells like a man who tells no lies
The waitress
    wants to kiss his neck
  irritate the rough curls there
she will probably fuck him hungrily later that night
none of them will plan on it
but a fever will grip them like leather

...and his lazy saunter out the door
will deprive her - remind her that it is
  Christmas and lonely
 that there will only be lewd
gold-tooth-capped attempts
 to squeeze her ass and crotch
matter-of-fact drunken requests
for a Yuletide blowjob...

she wants more than this
more than the muck festering on their dried hopes
will allow them to want
     maybe flowered gardens and fluffy pets
     a man who will plant fresh vegetables
and then knead his gnarled knuckles into her thighs
maybe a career as a nurse   an architect
     a man who will bounce her children on his knee
     a strong weathered looking man
     who will giggle silly with his daughters
     while she shakes her head in mock disapproval

...and this man she feels will grip her with a force
she has come to regard as comfort
he will talk to her - growl her name
beg for her fuck in the same deep cadence
love her well and hard
        He would kiss her forehead before leaving

...and he would leave   she knew
he would leave
     like the dancer left
     like the builder left
     like the one who loved her so much he cracked her
ribs and took her money   left
he would leave
     the cloying familiarity of her bed

her thick and willing lips
  the hot of her belly
  the non-stop cussing of her drunk aunt in the living
room
  the smoke of this bar
   the hopelessness of its tired randy whores speculat-
ing on his cock size
  the lazy cracking collisions of pool balls
  the juke box where another bitched-out bitter young
sister is playing Tyrone for the 17th time

she turns to fix a drink
and when she turns back
his glass is coming down on the formica counter
  the drink tossed back with the swagger of a Southside
gunman
He swallows effortlessly and leaves

        Love in a time of hopelessness
in the midst of an unforgiving Chicago cold is hard work
        even for one night
        so she runs into the fast falling dusk
feels herself collide with the brisk winter solstice
asks him   where he is going so soon

He calls her to him
  and she obeys like a familiar easy lover
he grabs her waist and pulls her to him
shoves his wide tongue into her mouth.
His thumb travels roughly up and over her engorged
nipple - fat as a thimble
  answers   -New York; I'll be back in May-

She knows disappointment intimately
  has learned to carry it like luggage
  returns to the bar

as easily as she submitted to his rudeness
Somebody has managed to wrest the jukebox away
A wailing Rasta proclaims something
     about not wanting to wait in vain...

She is aware of the cold
   her rib still hurts there at first frost
she is aware of the ominous toll
of the Salvation Army bell in the distance
     heads for the bathroom
     slips out of the black overalls
     and slides her fingers   two of them
   into her drawers   dewy with possibility
leans back onto the wall
   closes her eyes to capture the dark
and settles into the rhythm
     groaning
     and dreaming of spring

                                        Roger Bonair-Agard

Corporate Pricks
for C.P's everywhere-- we're comin' for you

so this is the end of the poetry slam
we've raised voices, praised choices
we've informed plans, formed clans,
my 'dyke,' your 'brother'
it feels strong to belong,
to exclude each other.
so while i'm tight with my girls—
my cunt speaks of fight
through its curls—
sometimes connection hides behind social divides,
factioned until obscure.
see, separate's not the cure.
and you say listen to her.
wasn't she boasting all that girl pride.
now she wants us boys on her side?
strutting the woman thang all night,
now she'll take muscle when it comes to the fight.
she'll welcome dicks
for battling
corporate pricks.

but see, the suit and ties,
they're on the hunt.
and getting screwed over doesn't equal cunt
cause if you're not rich,
you're just a part of the shit
and they're shovelling us up bit by bit,
flushing us down the corporate toilet.
and we say hey, it's ok to drown
down that middle road,
the less forboding road,
the 'hey, i vote, ok?' way,

please and thank you way,
lay down and roll over,
bulldoze me over way.
yes, it's a cinch from day to day
feelin rich, livin large and hearty—
at least you're in charge
of your tupperware party.

but i wanna propose we follow those
who chose a different way to knock.
those who banged with persistence
like the audre lorde's of my existence.
who chose a different way to walk—
took a chance, didn't prance, tiptoe,
twirl thru this world.
see, i refuse to slide past
even if it means coming in last.
i'm gonna stomp and rage and kick,
talk hard, think thick, you know it don't
take a dick to have balls. it don't take
balls to bust down the walls
of this cheap joint.
point is:

this whole country needs a cold shower.
we've forgotten we have power in
this mess, this cesspool of
dirty ideology— biology is destiny,
and all the other piss
taking the place of justice.
see there's a clean way to go, but
we're so covered in their scum
we've forgotten what we know.
so, let's wake up,
shake something up.
ask who's the pitbull in this

dog-eat-dog race,
who's clogging the system, who's the disgrace?
who'd sift through the money if i shit it in his face?
who's getting rich quick?
it's the corporate prick.
he's the one saying
"it's no fun supporting poverty through robbery
but why should i care
about losers on welfare?"
and he's saying, "sure i dig diversity-
it keeps those activists offa me,
i tell them get the fuck offa my back
as you can see my secretary's black."

and you're sitting there saying
conspiracy-theory is a thing of the past
and she's one of the last
to believe that rumor.
you say, "she's got no sense of humor"
so i try to find it funny
how the corporate pricks make money:
rape a nation: gain admiration
reap profit: no jail
rape your wife: easy bail
greed over need never seems to fail
in the corporate prick club

maybe that's it, the way it goes.
who knows?
maybe we should all put on ties,
try to rise to the top.
it doesn't take much strength to stomp
on some heads, learn how to say
"hey, it's the American way", with a smile
and have a knife in someone's back all the while.
cause now we can all slice up the american pie—

they say all it takes is a suit and a tie and a little couth
til you chip your tooth, realize your piece is fake.
guess we can't all eat cake-
there's just not enough dough in that batter
what's the matter is we forgot
it's not ever what it seems
when mr. corporate prick's baking our dreams.
cause it's not luck, honey,
that aint no four leaf clover,
see that money in his pocket
that's from screwing someone over.
all i'm saying is don't go
wheelin' and dealin',
it's your soul that Corporate Prick will be stealin'
as he calls you partner with a smile and a wink,
cause you're working together
to buy his wife's mink.
and even if you don't hand over the cash,
his stash relies on our complacency,
our lack of agency

and even writing this stuff isn't enough,
cause while we're impressing
with rhyme and repetition,
compressing politics into competition,
beating each other with words and soul,
it's corporate prick who's got the whole
picture. and i don't mock it-
who's got our paycheck in his pocket?
who's running these games,
who's calling the shots,
defining the names-
the haves, the have-nots,

see, it seems like it happened while we
were fighting each other—

me loving my dykes,
you embracing your brothers.

well, i'm gonna open my cunt wide enough
to stuff inside this human pride
we've collected.
because in this struggle we seem to
be connected.
i hear these souls in here,
we're growling like a pack of big bad wolves in here,
and we've smiled politely,
now we'll smile as we pound.
as we huff and we puff
and we blow this shit down.

Alix Olson

Reality
putting shit in perspective

Can you spare some change?
Can you spare some change?

Reality stepped up to me
while waiting for the train one night
      and asked for some change.

All woolly hair and beard   with long fingernails
resembling some unkempt, ethnic Jesus,
      he offered me his story.

    Bloodshot eyes reflected a possible future
    as I passed him a dollar bill.

He spoke of broken dreams   lost in a bottle,
using few words
        alcohol
        detox
        Bellevue
cutting like a knife through my fantasy.

In a flash I saw my own life
and realized how lucky I was
and realized how unsatisfied I was
      with that realization.

There were no thoughts of revolution then.

What is this revolution we envision if it will never reach
someone like him?
      Is there a poem we could write
      that would change his life?

What kind of poem
can put food into the hands of the hungry?
    What kind of poem
can put clothes on the backs of the poor?
    What kind of poem
can remove the despair from the heart of the broken?
    What kind of poem
can take away this feeling of helplessness
when I'm one paycheck away from being him?

And, if there were such a poem
where the hell would he go to hear it?

His bloodshot eyes are moist now
and I look down at my hands because
    there's nothing I can say to comfort him.

"I'm sorry..."
    For what?

        "Good luck..."
            Yeah, right!

            "God bless..."
                What God?

Mistaking my silence as his cue to leave
        he turns and walks away.

He claimed he hadn't bathed in awhile
    but the only stench left behind
    comes from me...

    Can you spare some   *change?*
    Can you spare some   *change?*
    Can you spare   *change?*

Can you   spare   change?
Can you   change?
Can you   change?

Can you spare some   change?

Guy LeCharles Gonzalez

Don't Think I'm Not a Nice Girl

for every wommin who has asked for permission to be an artist

so we've learned karate,
carry knives on our runs
wield words (like weapons),
prepare glares (hidden guns)
we've deconstructed, demystified
tried retribution, remythologized
we've been diagnosed with your diseases,
and still tried pleases, tried tears, tried Jesus.
you wanna see what it's like down here
in this pool of someone else's rules, well
jump in, take a swim or just sit in this pit
squishing bare toes in someone else's bullshit
we do it all the time.

still we've tried being patient,
collected, calm, nice,
trying praying, tried laying you,
paying the price
we've learned to scream
until our throats throbbed
what else do you do
while your cunt's being robbed.
and they say "you've made progress girls,
take a rest in-between,"
but see while you're resting,
someone else is progressing,
it's what i've seen.

so i take back the whispers,
the cute mute act,

and the high pitched giggles, yeah
i take them back.
i won't avoid your stare, evade your step,
nothing of that kind,
won't help you help me victimize
the only space that's mine.
see now i'd put my life on the line
just to see them trip,
frown and say "funny love, i never saw you slip."
i say, my life on the line,
you say "man, she's jaded."
i say, maybe control's
overrated.
like when we cackled, they called us witches,
now we don't giggle, they call us bitches
well i'm cacklin loud, taking it back, full of hiss,
cacklin proud now.

and they're getting nervous with this kissing each other,
scratching their heads,
"what's going on brother..?"
and they yell "feed your husband, stop feeding the fire!"
and we just cackle,
we're a fuckin witches' choir.
and we sing:
"sharpen your knives, sharpen your daughters
steam up the mirrors, bake up some dreams,
cook us some riots, fry up some screams,
and when you're sick of your skirts
slice open the seams"
cause they want domestics,
they'll give us needle and thread
for patching their egos.
we'll sow revolution instead.

and i see you saying subtle, sister,

less bite more bark
you can make your point without leaving such a mark.
subtle, sister, stop your seething,
i think we got it, i think we're even.

subtle like a penis pounding its target?
subtle like your hissing from across the street?
subtle like the binding on my sisters' feet?
subtle like her belly raped with his semen,
draped in his fuck, funny,
doesn't seem even.

see, sometimes anger's subtle, stocked in metaphor
full of finesse, dressed in allure
and sometimes anger's subtle, less rage than sad
leaking slow through spigots you didn't know you had.
but sometimes it's just

fuck you
fuck you
you see, and to me,
that's poetry too.

Alix Olson

art & the man
for curtis who never got to see me grow; and staceyann, whom I hope, will.

"the artist..." she tells me "is eons ahead of the man"
and when I hear this
   I think of Curtis' smile - continuous mischief
always playful and attentive
always ready in a crunch
      any danger; any adventure
how he might be glad that I had become 'artist'
  how the pain of his cramped closet
  the one my friendship with him kept
         shut and suffocating
 might have become a little easier to bear

      how his liver must have shredded inside
  as he joined our absurd teenage games
  the teasings and the drive-by stonings
      just so as not to give himself away
how that pain   and the bitter syrup he drank
         as he mingled it with his love for me
      might seem a sip sweeter

the artist has always been bane and darling
            protected by those we scorn
            abhorred by those we champion
Curtis wore me like a personal cross
  the thing under which he hid
  while he bore my cruel weight like a carcass
  to the hill of his own destruction

  We kept at this one-sided love
intersected by a woman whom we both loved
he; as a sister – I; in that new found worship of the flesh

we feted fought   made art and laughter
tight together in our joy for one another
  cramped together in the cannister
        of one another's denial

    so when Curtis disappeared for months
and my calls were answered only with
 'everything's alright; I'll see you soon...'
I'll be back in time to drink for Christmas
                in time to learn the holiday repertoire
                in time for all the important performances...
I thought nothing of his illness

...and when Marcia pulled up to my house screaming
to finally announce curtis' death
    by AIDS
I was not ready
        for the cruel pop-quiz of a self-examination
  the question recurring like an insistent fraction
would you have been his friend...?
    would you have been his friend if you knew...?
        would you have been his friend
if you knew he were gay?
...I still do not know the answer to that question
  only that I was never as good a friend as he deserved

Marcia fell into my arms that spring
  Curtis' phoenix energy no longer a buffer
  and she loved me   more than I deserved
Like any 'good' disciple   I denied Curtis
    when it appeared our association would fasten me
  to the cross of his imagined crimes
the punishable social court of his homosexuality
  and so escaped the bloody stigmata of his love for me

Sometimes I like to think...

as I wish for a time I cannot take back
and apologies I will never get to make
    that Curtis knew what Staceyann tells me everyday
     I hold her close
  safe in my choices and hers
"the artist is eons ahead of the man…"
and that he saw   in the short mandate of his years
that somewhere in my future   the man might catch up
    …and he decided right then and there to love me
    well before   I was worth it.

Roger Bonair-Agard

Behind the Music: the evolution of dreams...

I.

    In the 7th grade
dreaming under the influence of
    I Want My MTV!
when hip-hop was still for partying
and Hall & Oates ruled the charts
    I decided to learn the guitar
    12 year-old hormones assuring me
    this was the perfect way
    to get girls.

John Peter agreed.

We agreed on almost everything –
    Batman over Superman
    LL over Kool Moe D
    Robotron over Pac-Man
so when we signed up for strings
we both had visions of
money for nothing
and chicks for free
dancing in our heads.

On the first day of class
we learned to mistrust authority
finding a New York City public education
limited dreams to tradition
      left us to choose between
      the viola, violin, cello
        and bass.

Lacking any MTV reference point
but wanting to retain some shred of cool

jazz unconsciously imprinted on our hybrid genes
         we chose the bass.

         There were only three in the class
the third claimed by a kid nicknamed cockroach
before the final bell had rung.

We quickly planned our first video
scanned the class for potential co-stars.

II.

　　In the 7th grade
girls ruled the world
and she was Catherine the Great...
in that first-to-develop
breasts-and-hips kind-of-way
　　　leaving young boys goofy
　　　professing their love
　　　with songs they don't understand.

I wanted to do things with her
I'd only seen in movies
imagined her body leaned against my leg
fingers plucking at her strings
　　　her voice a low chord
　　　whispering my name.

John Peter agreed.

Her name has faded with time
　　　but the memory of that moment
　　　when she held up her hand
　　　　　– said she wanted to play the bass, too –
　　　stayed with me.

John Peter and I argued
like long-time bandmates
both ready to sacrifice our souls
convinced the reward would be a kiss,
　　　...at the least.

　　For the next two years
we played the cello
side-by-side
　　　third row back
　　　behind the violas

reading *twinkle, twinkle, little star*
from sheets yellowed with neglect.

Cockroach stood in the back
     – with her
plucking away from memory
        a low throb echoing
        in our hearts.

III.
Rock-star dreams fade
when exposed to the light of day.

    Years later
I'd hear someone say
there were more poets in the ghetto
    because guitars are expensive
    pen and paper cheap.

I remembered carrying home that cello
pressed against me like an unwanted sibling
on the rush hour 5 through the Bronx
adjustable leg loosened by time
threatening to put out an eye
    wishing that my load was
    a little bit heavier.

    Today, I write poems in low chords
        silencing the echoes
pen and paper less default than option
swearing my children will never
have to trade in their dreams.

Guy LeCharles Gonzalez

3 in a series for the Wildcat Woman
(because I miss Trinidad but I'm never going back)

(i)

what is ash wednesday,
when i am rocking
under a different rhythm's heat
to a sub-
terr
a
ne
an
beat
of off track, third wheel
bouncing
to electric engine room
rhythm sections?

    sections of my day lack the rhythm
    to be more than rote
extempo infractions forgotten
    my sins are unforgivable
conformity denies me the flair
to fly in the face of my demons.

(ii)

i want- a bassman, a tenor pan,
de engine room an' dawn ann in full flagrant swing!
i want to learn to ply rhythm,
like mih sister does fly waist-
with impunity.
- captured in this magic;

we does laugh
is you to ketch!
waistline an' riddim
unlike rhyme and meter
make no promises.

(iii)

i suspect that my skin petrifies
in rapid response to drops in temperature
no down jacket,
thick scarf,
ear muffs,
double gloves or hat
can tenderize surfaces
that desperately recollect hot
    stillness
of noontime Macqueripe with the softness
of anamnesis-

memory shredded by blades of frigid wind
and frosted to nebulous perfection
    in a cold that permeates souls.

Lynne Procope

Ill Legitimate

There was a rumble dumble
Five minutes it lasted
The mirror said
You are you conceited bastard

I am the ill
legitimate hot white son
of Hip Hop.
I am the bastard child
of the breakdance.
I slept on cardboard boxes to pay my dues.
I collected bottle caps
off spray paint cans
so I could pay my crews.

I learned how to backspin
from foster parents with black skin.
I won spelling bee-boy contests
with words like phat gold cable
and wrote book reports in rhyme
timed to a beat
I created with my fist on the kitchen table.

I battled armies at the Rink
with my square feet
and bare hands.
I made my last stand
a windmill pose.

I chose to moonwalk in circles
around my block.
The Roxy was the hotspot
but the streetcorner's where I learned to toprock.

I fought the topnotch. Wore this blood-red stopwatch.
Drew turntables with chalk on sidewalks
so I could play Hip-Hop Scotch.

I slept on the floor. People slept on my flow.
I crept in the back door
at late-night prom shows.
Heard the crowds oooohhh's and OOOO's
when I blew up the stage
in my pin-stripe lees and
my size five shell toes.

My head swelled
so I wrapped it in linoleum
to stop the spinning
when I watched the fake
wide grinning
from green white foes
with bright red faces
shouting "I hope you hang from those black fat laces."

Filling safe spaces
with traces of their be-fore fathers hate.
Taken from the pages of slave codes.
masters trying to trap slaves that trade codes.
Like slang signs
and gang signs
or gas-white-light hang signs
on the underground railroad.

The white foes
tried to snatch me
in the middle of a backspin.
They claimed me as their own
maintained that I'm the one they own.
said "don't roam

your real father needs you,"
said "it's not hate
it's just the way God made it,
then they tied me to a bed
and made me listen to Iron Maiden.

But I escaped.
I cut the nylon chords.
Put the CD player on pause.
Then jumped out the window
after I left my tag
in bubble letters across their walls.

Then I rose
from the ashes of a group home for wayward emcees.
That's where I learned
which way words look
trying not to be seen.

A family of microphone fiends
adopted me.
I got spotted
playing with metaphors and similes
in a sandbox.
Now my handlocks
when I grip a pen.
At first they thought I was a snake
because I shed my skin.
Then they saw how I could shake
that's why they took me in.

There was a rumble dumble
Five minutes it lasted
The mirror said you are you conceited bastard

Stephen Colman

Breathless

When I was young
I believed that if I held my breath while crossing bridges
I'd survive the day the ground gave way
plunging me into the dark waters below.

My mother would look back at me and smile,
How long can you hold it?

My silence was her answer
as eyes teared
and pulse quickened...

When I was young
I believed Batman
and Robin
and the rest of the Superfriends
really were on the other end of the phone
telling me it was past my bedtime
and that if I was good
and did my homework
and respected my mother
...that one day I too could be a superhero.

I never questioned Wonder Woman's deep voice
or Superman's gruff smoker's growl.

When I was young
I believed the skeleton in my closet
was the monster under my bed
so I confronted him
befriended him
called him poetry
and set him free.

When I was young
I believed I would one day change the world
through sheer force of will.

Manhood introduced me to bridges
        long and winding
where the ability to hold my breath paled in comparison
to the need to hold my ground.

Bridges collapse from neglect
            and acts of war
            or acts of God
a foolish game of semantics
no pen and ink hero could ever win.

I learned in time to cherish my mother's wisdom
and the true meaning of her words...

I still believe I can change the world
no matter what bridges I have to cross.

How long can you hold it? she asks.
        As long as it takes...

Guy LeCharles Gonzalez

i believe

i believe in jesus, i don't believe in his father
the hollow book, the holy crooks
or all their wholesome followers
i believe misogyny and patriarchy
are closet homo lovers
and they screw over their sisters
cause they're scared to screw their each other.
i believe harriet tubman should be on the dollar bill
we've had our fill of white boy faces,
time to change places.
i believe hilary, not bill, should have worn the crown
they could have learned from jack and jill,
which one would break it and fall down
i believe there are too many lonely lesbians
looking for a lover
and if some would lift their cool masks
maybe they would find each other
i believe people and products both need less packaging
cause bullshit is still bullshit
when you pull off all the wrapping
i believe people are see-through
if you hold em up to the light
i believe people are enlightening
if you plug em in right
i believe our system is a love affair between the up and
upper classes
cause it's easy to get screwed
when you're just raping all the masses
i believe diet coke is liquid steel
i believe too many women drink their meal
i believe in survival of the fittest
if you're ranking members of a gym
but if you're talking about the human club

you've gotta let everybody in
i believe art is universal
if you're a white straight male artist
talking to white straight men
i believe feminism's in reversal when we believe
art is universal cause then we're just believing them
i believe you should learn more than one language
you should learn to talk in tongues and lips
i believe in nipples and skin and toes and hips
i believe in noise from women's teeth and throats and-
cunts
the noise of poetry, music, laughter after screaming
cunnilingus
i believe women are sexy without makeup or clothes
i believe women are sexy when they're reciting prose
i don't believe in horoscopes, fortunes, fate, luck or
chance
i believe sometimes shit works out just cause of
circumstance.
so i believe if you call the wrong number
you should talk for a while
you might like 'em more than who you meant to dial.
i believe small talk is for small people
who have nothing much to say
if you really think it's so "nice out"
shut up and go enjoy the fucking day
i believe wall street invented the criminal mentality
the easter bunny laid heterosexuality
i believe that mutual masturbation makes a lot of sense
i don't believe in a white picket fence
i believe in picking fights and picketing riot dykes
i believe in loving in groups
i believe in loving alone
i believe in hardship, in travelling through hard shit
then i believe in coming home.
i believe some wives find their husbands boring

and they picture women naked
while those boys are snoring
i believe men need to revolutionize themselves
or they'll see
all those wives kissing jill sobule and me
i believe there are more buttons and more clever
bumper stickers every day
and less and less sticking to what they have to say.
more recycling of garbage, more recycling of cash
it all ends up in the same bin
with all the white corporate trash.
i believe there are too many babies
and too many weddings
and too many headings that started with Monica
i believe post-gay is presumptious,
just plain gay functions.
i believe that barbie should be used in anatomy class
as a perfect bag of bones, then taken to biogenetics
as an argument against clones.
i believe cell phone culture is ridiculous
imprisoning us in the cell of a social fetish.
i believe the worldwide web should be used
for the world's people and their web of movements
not for global companies
and their web of advertisement improvements
i believe baby dolls should have realistic clits
so baby dykes can start getting used to it.
and i believed the guy i waited on today who said
i'm one hundred percent nice i don't bite
i said i believe you sir and i'll take the beer
can you believe i'm one hundred percent queer
and i talk it and i teach it and i poet and i preach it
and i hold it and i mold it and i know it so i give it.
because i'm sure that i believe
i'm still learning how to live it.

legacy - bush tea lessons and manhood rites

My grandfather stood tall / five foot five to be exact /
wiry sturdy austere devout / He managed seven acres of
crop for 55 years, kept a grudge from age 8 till death, and
on the eve of his eighty-second birthday had enough
strength left / to chase 'stink mout' Martin / down the
street / because the boy had beat me up. He slipped off
his wood-soled slippers / picked up a bat on the run /
and at more than four-score years / scared the fear of
God / into a fifteen year old boy.
At family gatherings, he would reach into the sideboard
/ to pour me some 'chaka chaka' / he would call it /
unbothered with the specifics of liqueur, brandy, wine,
gin, rum / he'd invented his own collective noun / for
the stuff he said / would keep 'the cold' away.

Now, no more cocoa gets cut / coffee is danced only in
our nostalgias.

I exorcise my own demons now / my grandfather's body
/ unruined and previously unvisited / by doctor's or
dentist's wisdom / grins an unfamiliar grimace.

I grin along.

No more bush tea, fever grass or ground provision / my
grandfather inherits / a world of catheters and
chemotherapy / his pleasure relegated to / one daily
soaping and shaving.

I am not sure why this task is mine.

... but am told that with Juni in / the Cayman Islands /
I am at 14, the family's eldest male.

I shave him carefully -each stubbled strand greyed to perfection I slice smooth pulling his slackened flesh taut / against his sun burned skin. / The individual grey stubs / are luminous knobs of silver / gems of learning and wisdom.

My fourteen year old hands steady, I am proud of my skill with a straight razor / my grandfather is proud / to hand over his patriarchy at blade point / punctuating this new paragraph in our relationship, with proverb and information.

> *"The acre nearest the road is yours.*
> *It have cocoa an' tambran'..."*

> *"Talk some; keep some - everybody*
> *eh ready to know everyting ..."*

> *"Look some money in a kerchief in*
> *de drawer - yuh have your school*
> *books yet"*

I answer for the first time, dutifully / a sense of history / riding my shoulders in his stories and questions / the burden unsteadies my hand / dip the brush into the lather - camouflage for my hesitation ...
... and pick up the razor again / white-handled and deadly / I carve family jewels / knobs of silver - smooth / off his tightened black skin...

> *"...only drink bush tea."*
> *"Clean yuh teeth with Hibiscus branch..."*

In the final months before illness / like all people close to the land / grandfather prepared for his journey.

Though we lived on oblique corners / from each other /
he would go the entire block around / and
enter our back gate / so no-one knew where he went...

> *"...the land is divided in seven..."*
> *"Make sure yuh get yours..."*
> *"Watch out for yuh aunt, yuh sister, yuh cousin,*
> *who vex dat yuh gettin'*
> *anyting at all..."*

We would listen with supercilious reason / sure that
senility had finally come.

I bore his coffin at the funeral / the youngest of six pall-
bearers.

That Christmas I cried into the family festivities / the
razor's secrets at my breast pocket / my glass full of
'chaka chaka' / one tear / like the razor's fluid stroke /
strolling down my cheek / splashing rippling into the
beverage / echoing his proverbs.

Roger Bonair-Agard

children of a panman   an'a maswoman

overture

mamma is a maswoman
the best part of the high art -carnival
every metaphor for trini
she is the slow chip
early carnival monday morning
pronouncing the need to keep the beat,
the slow grind, and that sweet heat building

mommy is the dance to come
that will take all your strength and be worth the wait
- surreal as the purity of all white monday mas,
an' de gyalarrie of "watch me nuh"
a lesson to me of the
the value in both costume and flesh

she is a sweetness
hot sun shine, callaloo, macaroni pie and saltfish,
tuesday, high noon and glitter dus' makeup

she is de one who teach me how to play mih self,
    dance mih standard an' mih headpeice

she is the reason my brothers and i can sing off key,
out loud
and my sister makes laughter echo off people
like color off the grandstand stage at sunset

my mother is a maswoman who has carried color & joy
and the sudden, raging silence
of early ash wednesday morning with her
all of her life and mine

interlude

daddy is a panman,
and although i do not believe
that he has touched a tenor pan
with intent since before i was born

my father is a true panman,
from the days when panmen had was to fight
just to be dat
from dem other days when blackmen did used to fight
bajohn style an' ting
to know dis lil' bit ah space was theirs
    to be –lieve (bloods &cryps style) dat a black man
    could own, could belong

daddy doh talk too too much 'bout how dem was de days

he has perpetuated the bajohn myths in stolid silences
he will never tell the story of the
two foot long, full inch wide; battle scar
that dissects and connects his beautiful back-

he would give us music, all music,
    - ivory & steel,
invaders bomb competition style,
renegades steelban' in we blood;
lime in de panyard;

daddy gave me de music an' de riddim in my talk
dat fluid stretch in my stalk
i hear ol' time pan kaiso, and a bass man in my head
all de time, all de time i hear calypso music

    and i respect his silences
-value the stories he does tell

my father is bake an' shark
wid hot homemade peppasauce
every j'ouvert morning since ah born
his is the song
of all the handed down gifts of tradition
peas an' rice in de granstan for pre-lims
and the break in my step
when I hear the sweet clear roll of a tenor pan
when I stop to search for stories hidden in music

daddy is stability; the epicenter of community
panman and arranger

    my father is panman;
scarred and triumphant from de bajohn days

and he dreams music for his children

tempo

culture is second nature and the layer of skin that bleeds

shifting trickle beats from a well tuned tenor pan

ring out in dawn ann's
so slow   you   cyar   miss   me   walk
her laugh is a full throat a-minor
bouncin' off a rusty galvanize
her smile the barba green wide
 packed tight with history,
 your story,
 my story
you cyah tell her a damn ting
she cyar keep no secrets, not even her own
an' dem eyes always too wide
life wrapped too tight
dem eyes recordin'
every move , every sound ,
my sistah is always capturin' the nuances of life
 for instant replay when she reach home
raised in the music
and drama of a still shiftin',
now sinkin'island

tradition is the way you weigh truth,
reality and permanence

melody

and adrian will be a guitar pan
the rumble of unexpected melody
the sound of a steelband pulls him
farther away than it does, any of us
home - is a place he has mostly visited
in tall grass dreams of stray dogs & short fences
flyin' kite and playin' ketch
stonin' breadfruit trees
wakin' each day to another adventure

the traditions of trini hospitality
to him -   ingrained
but somehow, still new, the stuff of summer vacation
and every day in his brooklyn life...
adrian is a guitar pan
the unending joy
the challenge of the last child

joy because he is the angel of all our hearts
     because his name is a song in our throats
     because everything
     - is just short of what we want for him

challenge   because;
we all expect to correct our mistakes in him
          we do not expect him to make any of his own

family is the only truth we can ever own or create

counterpoint

guy is not music
    he is - undefinable as sound
        more; a strange silence
        even when he is all furious screaming
    he is - consistency
        that wall we truly know
        only in our subconscious
        he alone is certain of his needs

with a whole world that he should try,
he still creates it as he needs it to be
he is a peculiar silence and enigma to all of us
the challenge to love
despite the misgivings of history
the way i learned
that-   while everyone wants attention
some need it ....
and they blossom with the gift like the bouganvillea,
rich, colorful and more a part of me than i know.

nothing of where you come from ever leaves you.
more often it call you home.

carnival

and i am first born
not music i think,
only its child
i still do not know too many of my own truths
    no longer pause to consider reflections
    in my mirror
i am carnival- that time when the constraints of flesh
are suspended

a merging of color and costume and dance

i can be driving force in the dynamic
the tranquiltiy of the soul when -
all that is left of the dream
is the lift of your face to contrition
from the ashes of your sins

and i concede
i sometimes am like pan music
or at least like kaiso when dey write it for pan.

"when dem carnival children swing dey tail in de city
  dey sweet and the flouncy
  dey makin' life bouncy"

yeah sometimes da'is me- carnival

child of the children of a panman and mas woman...

Lynne Procope

Waiting for the Ibis

My Grandmother died
and I laughed—

Because she used to pee
in the street and tell stories about shooting nazis
from bell towers
with nuns
during lunch.

Because she greeted each morning
with a fart
and encouraged me to do the same.

My Grandmother died
and I smiled—

Because, "I am a socialist," she screamed
while pulling a knot of cash
from greasy pockets
stained by twelve hours at her restaurant,
neighborhood kids on bikes
snatching 20s from chapped, callused hands.

Because, "religion is bullshit,"
as she carved a verse
from Ecclesiastes
into hard wood paintings.

Because, "remember you are Muslim,"
as she lit a candle
in St. Patrick's Cathedral.

She wanted the Ibis

to carry her to a field of lentils and honey – to Egypt –
because her father-in-law
did not want his son to marry a gypsy woman – a Black
Woman.

Because Prague did not want her either
 – only Egypt could hold her –
tell her black and brown are beautiful.

My Grandmother died
 and I cried—

Because vodka blurs your vision
makes you snap heads
off little children,
your own children,
to replace your own head
filled with beatings and blows
by hands emptied of the impulse to hold
me.

You never did hold me,
scared I might hold back.

My Grandmother died
on a Sunday morning
gasping for breath
too weak to pee/paint/fart/snap heads/shoot nazis.

My Grandmother died
wide
awake
waiting for the Ibis
to take her to Egypt.

Stephen Colman

Sunday Mornings in the Kitchen with Gan'ganny

My grandfather was the king
of Sunday morning breakfast

up with the sun, we were teased awake by
the soulful sizzle of bacon and sausages
frying in their own fat and the sweet aroma
of homemade maple syrup with scrambled eggs
    and buttered grits

thick buttermilk pancakes and biscuits so fluffy
you'd almost forget the Bronx waited right outside the
kitchen window

his shockingly white hair – thick and defiant –
was always brushed neatly back
grease-stained apron tied tight around his waist
as he patrolled the kitchen like a general at war
      Aunt Jemima and friends
      never welcome at the table
    only family secrets
    and the sweat dripping from his brow
    seasoned our meals

he would tell stories of his childhood
complete with the hill that sloped upwards both ways
while hunting for squirrel or rabbit or deer
explain how they didn't taste much different from chick-
en
quietly slipping one or the other onto the menu now
and then to prove his point

I drew the line at scrambled cow brains
though I was always curious

whether he was pulling my leg
   or not

eventually, a cake would find its way into the oven
and we would be banished to the other side of the house
where my grandmother ruled with an iron fist
      and a thick, leather belt...

Years later and worlds away
just after high school and my grandmother's death
he and I shared a two-family house
in the too-green suburbs of Westchester County
with my mother, stepfather and brother

Sunday morning breakfasts continued
with a frequent glance in the backyard
where the sight of a deer would trigger recently buried
memories

I think I missed the Bronx almost as much as he missed
his Lula Mae

One night, when frustration and volume and tears
drove the final wedge between my mother and I
I sat in my locked room til well past midnight
waiting for my grandfather to go to sleep because his
bedroom was at the opposite end of the hall that led to
the front door

under cover of the bathroom faucet
I stuffed three bags full of almost
everything I valued into the trunk of my car
and started the asthmatic engine

returning to shut the faucet
his voice drifted down the hall

See you in the morning, he said.

I was a mile from the house
when I realized
it was a question...

Years later, when he died
I arrived late for his wake
eyes and throat moist from emotion and alcohol

our entire family had gathered
in the Bronx for the first time in years
and we reminisced and played catch up
trying to ignore the hanging question
of who would bring us together next

my mother and I exchanged tentative hugs
and I marveled at my brother's growth

Sunday mornings nowadays find me at the stove
more lieutenant-in-training than general at war
       me in charge of the eggs
       Salomé handling the biscuits
       Lynne frying the turkey bacon

I sneak Mrs. Dash past them both
while Aunt Jemima sits awkwardly at the table
and espresso brews in the automatic coffee-maker

some days, the eggs come out just right
and I can feel his hands guiding mine
and I can hear his voice come from down the hall

See you in the morning, he says

and this time
I know that it's not a question.

                        Guy LeCharles Gonzalez

Criminals
for model-citizens everywhere

They sat me down in the big green police chair
With a big green light cornering my soul.
They said:

"You tell us who's the boogey man, ma'am
Yeah, you point out the Criminal"

And they tell me they can tell I'm a
First-class, top-notch, jury-duty, law-abiding
Kind of chick.
So, I flash my big, bright smile, I say:

"Well, I'm glad that's what you think"

And they hand me a box of composites
Stacked in some kind of alphabetical caste
Where last names don't seem to matter,
Goes from A to Black to Blacker.
But I'm a model-citizen, yeah, and
Model-citizens don't cause kinks.
Yes, I'm a model-citizen
So I sit my top-notch ass down to think.

In the morning paper, they say:

"Those spam-eating spics
are out to scam your family.
Yeah, they'll rob your job,
soak up the last three drops in this
Trickle down, down
Down-under country"

Well, big-business takes its little piggies to market
By keeping us dependent,
But the morning paper says
The Criminal
is the Immigrant.

And on the four o'clock pop-rock talk show, Joe says:

"Yeah, a dyke is easy to spot.
She looks like a man, talks like a man,
acts like a man, yeah
But she's sure as hell not"

And all the other guests say:

"Yeah, Joe, I think she's out to get your woman"
And by five o'clock, all the other Joe's in America know
The Criminal
is the Lesbian

And on the TV News, it's:
"Poor Black Women- colon- The Expert Opinion"
And all these white male scholars saying:

"Well, she shouldn't have a baby if she can't feed him.
But she shouldn't have an abortion either,
She should just know better.
You see, knowledge is power"

Yeah, but power is money and
Money's what matters.

And in the New York Times, it's
handcuffed protestors in Seattle
And the headline reads:
  "Angry Activists Start a Battle"

And the World Bank Leaders and the WTO
And Disney and Visa and Mansanto
And Goodyear and Texaco
All smile and say:

"Sure is nice to own the paper on a day like today"

So, I'm sitting in the big, green police chair
With a big, green light cornering my soul.
They say:

"You tell us who's the boogey man, ma'am
Yeah, you point out the Criminal"
So I finger the composites stacked in my hand,
I flash my big, bright model-citizen smile.
I say:

"I'm sorry Sir.
But the Criminal
Aint in this pile".

Alix Olson

cicatrix

the creeping tissue of my scars
fills me with wonder

how my flesh heals with a hard wall and regret
how my hand shakes when i forget to hold myself more
tightly
forget to brace my self against any jarring of these scars

a deep red cord racing along the pit of my womb
whips in a thick line from the base of one hip bone
swells to anticipate my lovers' fingers
just before the point of the other

    it reminds me that the muscles in my stomach
    are bound in fine threads,
    hand stitched like a pre natal quilting bee
    the threads will dissipate
like the whispers of women who tell
tall tales of childbirth
like the years when i knew i wanted babies.

i have resolved not to be cut again,
never to swell with his child
and i cannot explain this as some blithe discarding of
mores and stricture
nothing in me rebels at the idea of marriage or is
repulsed
by a head pressed to a mother's breast

i have understood love cupped into my partners palm
and seen the reflection of my womanness hooded in the
curve of his hand to my hip
    he told to shave my head if i wanted

take all risks that i dared
never promised to catch me when
i fell

but he stood aside and watched me flail
knelt beside me and smiled, offering his hand
brushing my bruises
kissing my aches
promising my cuts would heal
into battle scars that i could be proud of
   - he never imagined that i would lie down
   before this knife

i am woman enough to know the marks left
by this cutting away will not fade
and i have been all things to myself for long enough
to treasure the aching of fresh wounds,
the familiarity of scars.
what i need to remember is that this mark makes me
more whole
the cicatrix really is like a badge of battle
and i am winning myself back again,

yearning in soft places
for the screaming ache of our progeny
but i will never turn back the healed lip of my skin
and the woman i am becoming
will never be thin or really afraid again

i am choosing my marks and tattooing
my dreams for perpetuity
   easing into my bed alone
   easing into this life alone
smoothing sweet oil into the hard scars on my womb
- i check my mirror for signs of healing.

Lynne Procope

Mother's Book: found poem

"Mother's Book," 1831,
knows best.
The use of flannel-drawers,
provoking irritation,
is useful for inviting
the flow of the menses.
We should advise
gymnastic exercises,
walking and riding,
the games of battledore.
At last resort,
leeches to the vulva.
Menstrual exhaltation!

Home economics textbook, 1954,
knows best.
Have dinner ready.
Most men are hungry when they come home.
Prepare yourself.
Put a ribbon in your hair and be fresh looking.
His boring day may need a lift.
Prepare the children—
they are little treasures.
and he would like to see them
playing the part.
Greet him with a warm smile.
Make him comfortable.
Suggest that he lie down in the bedroom.
Let him talk first.
Try to understand his world of strain and pressure.
Make the evening his.
There will be a test!

Bloomingdale's christmas catalog, 1996,
knows best.
Treat your little ones to a treasure
for hours of make-believe fun.
Our boy's trunk includes
hat and play knife in pouch,
bandanna and vest,
and saber and eyepatch.
Our girl's trunk includes
a silver tiara,
pink satin conical hat,
lavender glitter cap-sleeve leotard,
rainbow net tutu with rose buds,
solid pink boa,
pink glitter cape,
 mock pearl necklace,
and tape of the "12 Dancing Princesses" story.
Or order our newest Barbie:
CK gray crop top, and
black bra and panties.
All American made by A Wish Come True!

Alix Olson

144

Jennica – the anti-barbie

in their perfect barbie doll house
by their perfect barbie doll sea
they got ready to have the perfect barbie doll child

the summer of love a distant memory
they rutted in the early eighties
Reagonomics   Thriller   the birth of spandex
the child was born   perfect barbie doll child

they both had the perfect barbie doll name for her
Dad wanted Jennifer   Mom liked Jessica
so they dubbed her in compromise
blonde blue-eyed and absolutely American
they called her   *Jennica*

she is the darling   of barbecues
 and power-lunch play dates
the perfect marriage of the perfect middle-america
names

but it's a funny thing the spirits have in store for us
all the religions' tricksters conspired on the laugh
Coyote Elegba even Judas joined the fray
and the child decided on the first day of kindergarten
on that first occasion that little barbie doll boys will hit
barbie doll girls
  she broke free

who knows – maybe the boy's name was Ken
he walked up smiling
she offered her ice-cream cone
he punched her – the cone fell
he ran off giggling

and she   always the correct barbie doll girl   cried

later that afternoon
she stabbed him in the eye with a pencil
the counselor's report said:

>   *unusual rage
>   *preternaturally vicious

  her parents are chagrined

but Jennica was finally born
  finally realized that old native tradition
of renaming oneself to change one's destiny

decided on karate lessons instead of ballet
      soccer instead of cheerleading
      carpentry instead of french
    wanted the summer job at the drugstore
the one where the cute boys went to buy condoms and
KY jelly
instead of the boating trip to Mexico

she learned to tie the perfect half-hitch
  marched on Washington
wore the black floor-length skirt and hiking boots
to the prom
floor length blonde hair
corn-rowed knotted at the waist
Free Mumia   lipsticked on her cheeks

no-one's suburban housewife she refused jennifer
no-one's dumb blonde kitten she killed jessica
became her own life-sized fully automated
5 ft 11   160 lb action figure   *jennica*
    complete with a kung-fu grip

so I walk up to her register
see her name tag   and fancying myself clairvoyant
say to her
-...guess your parents couldn't decide
 on jennifer or jessica-
and she answers:
-why, have you seen that name before?...-
and her eyes light up
softening to the hard mascara on their edges
hoping for a moment that somewhere
  another jennica has survived
the barbie doll hazing of her unfinished youth

because anywhere we bear the burden of our destinies
we hope for kindred spirits
patron saints of our cause to guide us through
we practice our suffering with the stoicism of martyrs
and hope strangers will guess at our purpose
name us anew
and bring us to some new realization
wearing our rage in our passions
and our viciousness in the intensity of our love

Roger Bonair-Agard

Daughter of the Revolution
Peruvian Embassy, Havana, Cuba – 1980

for Salomé

in her dreams
she cries out my name
under cover   unconsciousness
    fear of loss
    found lurking
    in shadows
she dreams me   gone
silhouetted against the past

iron gates scaled for freedom
fists and bats raised in tyranny
the fatherland engulfs her mother's name

echoes in her mind...

five year-old eyes search
huddled masses of hope
and despair

contradictions collide
cling to mother's tired legs
the stench of decay
ripe in tender nostrils
    separation sharp
    in her throat

dry lips cannot refuse
the sustenance of a saltine
taken from bruised hands

a father returned
bent but not broken...

    years later
separated again
the search for freedom taking different forms
scar tissue   still sensitive
fear lingers like a first love

freedom a limited resource
fear always in abundance
resolve a delicate figurine
    encased in glass...

    we poets profess
american in our ignorance
    savor the foreign delicacy
    the exotic metaphor
    the hollow call

more willing to spill ink
than blood...

she has lived it
breathed through pores
clogged with piss and shit
until her skin sweats it out
    her soul screams
    and the dreams come again...

these times
her body shakes softly

these times
her breathing flows faster

these times
her silence is frightening

...i pull her close
whisper that i am there
that i will always be there...

some revolutions are small
a single soul in the balance
    and i will die before losing this one

Guy LeCharles Gonzalez

the healing

(i) returning to the arms of the man
       who had left her most scarred she
did not at first hear the desperate screaming.
pedestrian aches returned to resonate,
the wailing faded into sunsets
that lingered longer
each day in the coming.
the wailing came from somewhere so far beyond her
that her face did not feel the trembling of pain
in the air of that damply dying house
and the sunsets came only in inches
          during that summer season of disquiet.

(ii) a marrow deep alone visited with her bruises
       in a house so crowded with her fear
that she loosed her grip on sanity, for brief morning
moments as she scoured the prison
that pretended to be her home,
which intended to be her grave.

she scrubbed darkly ruined skin
imagined her heart quivered full;
imagined her body resonated
more exacting emotions than an
unsettled collusion of fear, hate and the serrating need
to believe that she was wanted.

(iii) battered in to yet another miscarriage;
        she left running.

(iv) but there are no safe houses, even in the arms of
        family after years of shared life.
so she skipped meals,

haunted bus depots ,
grappled with despair and her relentless shattering
a suitcase torn at the base,
in danger of tumbling her dreams.

(v) when she was long gone,
     far from all men who had ever loved her
from her fickle heart longing to pitch itself
into the fray of
one
more
abrading embrace
then distance taught her heart to cherish self again,
distance-
and the crucible of a womb hollowed so thin
that screaming had seeped in and taken refuge.

so now she welled up with the source of that sound,
now she heard it rushing up
and pushing at the roots of her teeth
in her final acquiescence-
she rocked herself out of the corner,
she rocked herself;
arms wrapped close about her head, she rocked-
knees curled to her breasts, she rocked;
balanced upon only precarious curves, bare heels .
she rocked
and she screamed
    -as she never had before
and the rush of blood,
chipped bone, endless bruising, forfeited freedoms and
stolen smiles -
seethed to a flashflood; spun her on the axis of her spine
which was long and curved to a flinch,
where it ebbed;
leaving the residue of her soul,

the dried bed of her body -
a serengeti waiting to rejoice.

(vi) now deep in the marrow of her soul, she is alone-
       not recognizing the woman sitting beside
her self in the summer, sunning her scars,
reasoning her healing has not come easy
seasoning newly supple flesh
taking emotions as they approach,
to capture them for the savored taste,
the fragrant freshness of feeling
a burn that lingers with an aftertaste of self.

it is a flavor she senses in the aftermath
       of the screaming
       in the resonance of her healing.

tasting self
she has come up out of her crouch in the corner
stretching for the doors;

bleeding a little with every step.

Lynne Procope

155

Alvin Ailey Dies Everyday

Screams from the apartment below
flow up the airshaft in staccato rhythms
salsa, spanglish and struggle.

For the third time this week
Angelica and Emmanuel spar verbally
the occasional punctuation of flesh against flesh
demanding my attention.

The music masks the words
bounces off untrained ears
my feet tap a discordant tune.

Salsa, spanglish and struggle
demanding my attention
my feet tap a discordant tune.

Glass crashing against wall
flesh smashing against flesh
words thrown carelessly into the air
become truth.

The music gets louder
as words sharper than glass fly through the air
like shrapnel.

Demanding my attention
flesh smashing against flesh
as words sharper than glass fly through the air.

She stands in the hallway
eyes closed so tightly they tear
she dances to the ever-louder salsa

arms outstretched towards an imaginary partner.

I've never heard them say her name
only, "Your fucking daughter"
and, "I wish she was never born!"

As words sharper than glass fly through the air
she dances to the ever-louder salsa
and, "I wish she was never born!"

The ambulance screeches to a halt
sirens blaring and lights flashing
neighbors bow their heads
their shoulders slumped.

Her small body lies still
under a simple white sheet
never to dance again.

Screams from the apartment below
For the third time this week
The music masks the words
Salsa, spanglish and struggle
Glass crashing against wall
The music gets louder
Demanding my attention
She stands in the hallway
I've never heard them say her name
As words sharper than glass fly through the air
The ambulance screeches to a halt
Her small body lies still.

Guy LeCharles Gonzalez

Witches

for my grandmother, Dorothy Zager Katz who won
nine gold medals in the Senior Olympics

they've made us fear every year,
every extra hair that sprouts on tit or chin
til we begin to forget the wisdom we've collected,
til we've defected to the 'distinguished' older men
and they win— again.
well, i've decided to trade their old lady prescription
for a witch revolution that defies description,
yes, this hag will ride her wrinkles to the sky.
when i'm an old witch
i'll be ready to fly.

i'll just saddle up my saddle bags
one pouch for each thigh, pack em with pride,
yeah, grip my thick sides and ride.
i'll grasp my broomstick with a gnarled knuckle
buckle in each saggy tit, then fuck that, i'll say
these fat witch titties hurt today
and they'll wiggle loose and alive.
and as my broomstick rises,
i'll shake my hips like tambourines,
alarming little boys with the noise of my shaking thighs
in the skies above
and all the while, the little girls will smile
cause they'll know the music
of sisterly love.

and it's funny how they say an old cunt
should be all dried up
cause i'll give myself a lube job
shake my broomstick til my clit throbs
til i sing into the winds the unpredictable desire,

the unfathomable fire
of self-loving passion.
til i scream the screams unnoticed
of rapes unwitnessed,
til i moan the moans of wives accosted
by "boys will be boys" who just lost it for a moment.
the groans of all those moments running together
into some woman's forever.
yes, i'll rise with the song of the witch unleashed,
this bitch barking wild, this woman-child,
this tight-ass cunt uncoiling
at the sight of the cauldron boiling...

see, in that sky we're gonna cause some trouble,
make a little Dick Stew bubble—
we'll need the tongue of a liar or two,
some Phil Knight or some Rudy should do,
a dash of Rush Limbaugh, i thought
a cup of Ronnie Reagan on top,
that slop is bound to trickle down.
a Wall Street boy, a CEO or two,
they can downsize all day
while they're merging in our stew--
and then eye of Newt too,
and all the other nasty white boys—
the military, the budget, some of their toys
to keep 'em quiet while they're brewed,
you know Newts when they riot
they're downright rude.
and i'll keep stirring up my pot,
stirring up my plot to throw in any man
who puts his hands on my sister when she says no
who's lookin "tasty" now, mister,
In you go!

and i'll be flying.

i'll have my hands in my hair,
i'll grasp the gray, pay homage to its journey
stroke my leathered skin, full of fight and fury
weathered by the storms of audre lorde,
the rage and glory that hover
by stories of sisters loving each other.
and i'll spot a boy scout
helping a granny across the street,
feeling manly and strong,
til this Witch Charming comes along.
i'll sling my tits like grenades
to the ground, they'll anchor me down.
i'll whoop and howl like jane,
swing down on a varicose vein,
unfold my stomach rolls for red carpet,
my royal landing to the street
i'll sweep that granny off her feet,
make room on the back of my broom
and we'll rise to the skies, two witches
surrounded by sisters soaring through roaring storms,
thunder clouds obscuring vision,
but we'll know our mission:
to keep riding high.

so i can't wait 'til that day i make my cane
my broomstick,
sweep myself off my own two feet,
pick out all my false teeth and grin-
til i'm like mother jones or harriet tubman,
like ivy botini or emma goldman,
like dorothy zager katz or emily dickinson,
like sojourner truth or lucille clifton.
til these bones are in their crone prime
and at that time i won't grow old with a lady's grace,
won't look in the mirror at my wrinkled face
and sigh or groan or cry
because i'll be looking at the face

of a proud old witch
who's finally ready to fly—
see, all that hocus pocus shit
is just to scare you away, brother
cause real witch magic
is just sisters
loving
each other.

Alix Olson

I Don't Love You

I don't love you
in that,
"I'll walk through fire for you" way,
in that,
"your love keeps lifting me higher" way.
I don't fear the pain
of possible rejection
or feel a tug at my heart
when you're gone.
I don't think of you
when I listen to love songs.
I don't love you
in that,
"I'm gonna write a book of poems about you" way.
This might be the only poem you get.
I don't love you
In that,
" I can't find the words" way.
My body doesn't sway
when I hear your name.
My knees don't shake
when we make love.
I wouldn't drive more than 2 hours to see you.

But I love you.
Just not in that way.

I love you in passing.
I love you like the smile
you sometimes flash
hints at happiness.
I love you without thinking,
like blinking.

I love yo in the way
one of your front teeth is gray—
the color of my love for you.
I don't miss you when you're away.
I love you most
when I'm looking.
I love you like how
Martha Stewart loves cooking.
I love you in a slow way,
in a you never know way.
I love you in those ways,
so then this way
I'll know
that when your love does
start lifting me higher,
when I start getting hot
from walking through your fire,
I will really mean it when I say
"I love you... in that way."

Stephen Colman

religious sex: or how to tell your boys about the night before

...her body was flawless -
every angle I looked at
 was a lyric
                como una palabra precisa
her 'ooohs' and 'ai papis' - like her pedantic rantings
were melodies

She didn't move - mira
she was movement
              met her at a club; you know the club
where los morenos become Africans once again
and el merengue is in calypso beats
 and the sistas, que lindas - the sistahs

are sopping up salsa beats in the sweat of frilly under-
wear letting the heart of the congas trickle back down
their legs from their...   so anyway - there she was

 killing me on a drum
                her hands twirling
 coming back down in syncopation
with the outside swing of her hips   *y confieso*
I   *how you say?*   lusted a bit
thought maybe I knew how to love again

porque
she knew a secret
the secret
that the beauty of la música she created didn't belong to
her
not that 'we are the world' shit - coño

pero que la música... es del mundo

so all her movements were round
and her eyes were closed and if you looked close
you could actually see the salsa
                    wet and dripping   leave her hand
and fly out above the crowd

we all applauded when the band was done
and a few brave chicos
stepped forward to help her from the stage
    she was still sweating
and the salt was rolling off her body
crashing loud to the ground   como las maracas
as she came to me   porque papi
I knew where the sound of the maracas
was coming from
I knew how to get guitar strains
 off the high riding hardness of her nipples.

        We sucked things without names that night
and danced naked in her one-room apartment
to una canción en nuestras cabezas
Isn't that where all the canciones are?
We danced naked   facing her altar
 to Ochun y Chango
we were still sweating
the salt was still making maracas music on the floor
around us
she took my hand
            "Papí, dame la mano" - she said
and she put it -   down there
and she brought it   -to my lips
            "Don't stop talkin papí..."   -
 and my words became canciones again
y bailamos...

and we dance...
and she whispers...
      "never forget where la música comes from papi
      "never forget where la música belongs -"
               " - *te amo*"

Roger Bonair-Agard

latter-day saints
for Willie Perdomo and Imani Springer

I. 1996

–I am you. You are me.
–I am you. You are me.

perspective flipped
god taps me on my right shoulder
whispers in my left ear

–I am you. You are me. We the same.

his words communion wine
his voice   a deep, husky red

–I am you. You are me. We the same. Can't you feel our veins
   drinking the same blood?

i swallow deeply
inhale the scent
of prophecy

II. 1997

   he says
if it wasn't for her
I would be standing on the corner
thinking about the world
drinking blackberry brandy
keeping a cold hustler company
with stories from back in the days

and I know exactly what he means

if it wasn't for her
i'm not sure where i'd be now
but back then
when dreams became nightmares
you'd find me in a bar called botanica
borrowed pen in one hand
cold pint of stout in the other
american spirit hanging from my lip
       unable to change my world
       determined to change everyone else's

i wrote it all down
alternately angry
       drunk
       suicidal
       revolutionary
       drunk
       alone

despair is the muse of the blocked and
i was prolific

III. 1998

where he's from
a nickel costs a dime

langston told him that

where i'm from
trees are few and
far between

leaves, like dreams of escape
wither, die, fall, float
in curbside streams to the sewers below

no one told me this exactly

but i could hear it in his voice
when he tells me what his mother said,
"Bueno, mijo, eso es la vida del pobre."
(Well, son, that is the life of the poor.)

when we finally met
on the other side of
our own books of Job
he stepped down
from the pedestal i'd placed him on
shook my hand,
   god becoming man
   to save my soul

IV. 1999

a twelve-year old poet
asks me
why I do not write anything funny

eyes aglow with innocence and hope
i do not have the heart
to tell her that i lost my sense of humor
years ago
but my poems
have told her exactly that

she smiles at my hesitance
and i want to tell her about

every single thing
that has ever stolen my faith
wish there was a way
to put it all in one poem
shove it down people's throats
make them choke on it - gag for air
beg for second chances
       to do things right

but i don't

in her eyes
is the hope i'd lost
and she offers it to me
no strings attached
       just a simple question
       and a smile

V. 2000

of all the books
resting on my shelf
what i remember most are the voices
and the people they belong to

–I am you. You are me. We the same.

there is no poem
that can change
our worlds

only poets
who can change
our minds

Contains excerpts of Nigger-Reecan Blues; Reflections on the Metro-North, Winter 1990; and, Where I'm From by Willie Perdomo, WHERE A NICKEL COSTS A DIME (W.W. Norton, 1996).

Guy LeCharles Gonzalez

incantation for a poem

pick the words you want to sing, then
throw them like truth from project rooftops,
watch them fall-   bodied thick and dark,
    full grown words; when pitched just right
    have an aura of innocence. they buck;
    desperate to find some purchase, to
reach some solid thing,
flail;   praying their reality is altogether different.

    your words acquiesce to their destruction and you
watch the howling denial of their passing ease
    into a singing
watch your sweat dry on the flat planes of their meaning
listen- for the sibilant sighs their pain makes,
wonder at the way their weeping sounds like laughter,
wonder at the way their weeping sounds.

remember the joy those words once gave you,
reach for them at 2am
    your flesh will touch only your cold, used up pen
    never look again for where the fall.
    you- are the only point to impact.

    and you
draw these bloodied words slowly
    up a stairwell behind you
huddle with them around failing heat
    in a building built on the brink of an abyss
    when those words rock you to sleep,
dream in defense of your truths,
scheme to induce magic and salvation
feel the words quiver in your hands
    slews of words in luminescent strands

listen close to the sorrowed rising singing that separates
    hues and
    cry
listen- still as they sigh, when none will understand
listen close-
    when words are born in buildings
    built on the brink of an abyss
    you never see, when they start to fall
    - from windows banked for safety
    by government checks
    onto streets weighed down by over anxious luxury
    and onto backs branded and enslaved
    by the casual ownership
    of too many things

    your words can turn their backs on you
    and dive without your asking
    they can leap into the abyss
    crippled by flawed and broken wings
    strapping labels to their backs
    like straight jackets for sanity.

    your words like your brothers can find the abyss
    from which you   once   fought   back
    it invites them in, knows each one by name
    calls them out from your fingertips
    and bodies bucking, limbs flailing desperate
    for purchase
    your words will drag you along to their end.

      and your screams will turn
    day by emptied day to singing,
    the screaming
    will turn to singing which will turn upon itself
    and then those songs will ease   - to humming
    and here, you must

listen well
anticipate the verse

the screams will turn to singing
and the songs will turn to humming
and that humming,
that easy acquiescence to a death

that humming

which lingers in your ear
that humming;   indicting
and raw as damage to your brain
there
that-

that is your poem.

Lynne Procope

I can't bear these accounts I read in the *Times* and elsewhere of these poetry slams, in which various young men and women in various late-spots are declaiming rant and nonsense at each other. The whole thing is judged by an applause meter which is actually not there, but might as well be. This isn't even silly; it is the death of art."

Harold Bloom

Burning Down the House

An Afterword by
Guy LeCharles Gonzalez

Faced with the surging popularity of spoken word and the poetry slam, The Academy of American Poets, long known for its gala reading series, was forced in 1995 to reevaluate its approach to their mission of creating a wider audience for contemporary poetry. "[We] certainly could no longer claim to be an innovator in this regard," says William Wadsworth, executive director of the Academy. "Looking at how much emphasis was being put on the performance aspect of poetry, I came to feel that it was the Academy's proper role, as an institution, to do whatever it could to reinforce the book of poems."

After a year of planning, the Academy launched National Poetry Month in April of 1996. The event rolled into bookstores, all aglow with its mission to "foster an appreciation" for poetry among the masses. In 1999, its fourth year, bouyed by a media blitz bigger than ever, National Poetry Month claimed over 90 sponsoring organizations and promotional tie-ins that include everything from the distribution of 40,000 books of poetry by Volkswagen to a special issue of *Poets & Writers Magazine*.

A noble mission, no doubt, but there are many that look on with a smirk and wonder, *What took them so long to realize the need for something new?*

Fifteen years ago at the Get Me High Lounge in Chicago, Marc Smith, construction worker by day, poet by night, decided he'd had enough of the status quo. He'd grown tired of the stale politeness of the academic poetry reading, where the poet was placed on a pedestal and had no obligations to his audience other than to

179

show up and read poems. His solution: empower the audience - take poetry down from the tower and not only make it available to the so-called masses, but make it answer to them. Thus was born the poetry slam, a grassroots vehicle for fostering an appreciation for poetry year-round. In the years since, despite often harsh criticism from the academic world, poetry slams have sprung up in nearly every major city and several smaller ones, both here and abroad.

This revolution against the establishment is not unique in the history of poetry. "When Ezra Pound and TS Eliot came along," says Wadsworth, "there were a lot of poets who thought the world had gone to hell. The values changed. A new generation came along and really changed things. That's always the case. I'm sure there were poets who were upset when people started writing in English instead of in Latin."

Since the advent of slams, the spoken-word movement has offended the sensibilities of the establishment on several fronts, not the least of which has been its insistent democratization of the art form. In the slam, anyone can get onstage to read a poem – and the standards of quality rest entriely on the subjective appreciation of randomly chosen members of the audience, who rate poems, Olympic scoring-style, from 0 to 10. Academia's seal of approval is neither required nor sought.

"Back in Chicago," remembers Patricia Smith, four-time National Poetry Slam Champion, as well as an award-winning journalist, "there were pundits in the academic world that said [slam] would never last and it would be the death of poetry. [It] began to get a lot of attention, audience and press without being 'sanctioned.' No one was able to 'discover' slam. It birthed itself. It grew despite no grant money, no kissing ass, not worried about being published..."

Charles Bukowski, arguably one of the most influential antiacademic writers of the last century and an honorary "slam" poet, wrote in 1990:

> to disrupt this sanctuary
> is to them like
> the Rape of the Holy Mother.
>
> besides that, it would also
> cost them
> their wives
> their automobiles
> their girlfriends
> their University
> jobs.

The irony was that many of these "slam" poets, were no different from those that saw them as barbarians at the gate, simply seeking a forum for their voices to be heard.

Brenda Moossy, an MFA student at the University of Arkansas and a successful slam poet and organizer in the Ozarks, always incorporates her work in slams into her classes. "[It] gives permission for people to think outside the box, allows for creative leaps and jumps...lets them see that everyday language and experience are very valuable and, in fact, at the core of what poetry is about."

"Poetry itself is revolutionary," says Bob Holman, who went from directing the readings at the St. Mark's Poetry Project in the late '70's in Manhattan to creating the slam scene at New York City's Nuyorican Poets Café in the early '90's. "To write a poem, even to read a poem, to take on all that language can give you is to become an activist. To get the poem to people in this world, you have to utilize the mechanisms that this world provides."

One of those mechanisms is America's fascination with competition.

"In the history of poetry," says Wadsworth, "a lot of classical or ancient traditions included the same principle, competition between poets; it was judged in one way or another but it was very much like a competitive sport. Slam has roots that go all the way back in the oral tradition."

And yet, one of the major criticisms of slam is its competitive aspect. Many in academia decry the thought of poems dueling on stage for the approval of an uncredentialed audience. SlamNation, last year's award-winning documentary of the 1996 National Poetry Slam by ESPN-producer, Paul Devlin, sparked controversy with its tagline: "the Sport of Spoken Word."

The father of the slam, Marc Smith views such objections as hypocrisy of the highest order. "Poetry in [academia] is competing all the time," Smith says. "You compete for editor's approval, for admission, and it's a closed competition. [There is] more competition in MFAs, more serious, more cutthroat than there ever could be in the slam world. Most slammers realize [slam is] just a format, a mock-competition, a drama that makes an audience focus its attention."

Another frequent criticism was that so-called "slam" poems did not function on the page. Jonathan Galassi, editor-in-chief of Farrar, Strauss & Giroux once called slam poetry "a karaoke of the written word." More recently, noted literary critic Harold Bloom referred to it as "the death of art."

Times have changed - the slam has proved itself a viable art form, and many of the poets who got their start there have proven their abilities both on stage and on page. Paul Beatty, Maggie Estep, Willie Perdomo, Crystal Williams, Carl Hancock Rux and many others have became major voices in contemporary literature.

"Like it or not," says Wadsworth, "this is what's going to bring this art form into the 21st century. I think it's the creation of a new genre, the creation of a new music. How it evolves will be very interesting."

Bukowski said it best:

>we have come from the alleys
>and the bars and the
>jails
>
>we don't care how they
>write the poem
>
>but we insist that there are
>other voices
>other ways of creating
>other ways of living the
>life
>
>and we intend to be
>heard and heard and
>heard
>
>in this battle against the
>Centuries of the Inbred
>Dead
>
>let it be known that
>we have arrived and
>intend to
>stay.

Walt Whitman once said, "To have great poets, there must be great audiences." And that audience is growing. Ten years ago, the first National Poetry Slam was held in San Francisco, California, a one-night event as part of the now-defunct International Poetry Festival. Two teams of poets, from San Francisco and Chicago (with Paul Beatty, an MFA student from Brooklyn College, representing New York), sparred verbally before a crowd of over three hundred people, the festival's biggest turnout. In the summer of 1998, the ninth annual National Poetry Slam in Austin, Texas featured 45 teams of four poets each, from the US and Canada, participating in four nights of non-stop poetry, which culminated in a finale witnessed by a standing-room-only audience of over thirteen hundred people.

Marc Smith reflected on his creation: "Every revolution becomes an institution. Though it's being adopted in academia, the main movement is still very radical. It's still fresh and evolving. The mission isn't anywhere near completed."

That mission – making poetry accessible, providing a platform for all voices to be heard – is one that will not take place in the aisles of your local mega-bookstore one month a year. It will not be sponsored by Nike, Sprite or MTV. It is not wedded to the elitist posturings of academics holding on to their tenures for dear life. It is a year-round process that is happening in coffeehouses and bars and community centers throughout the world.

The match has been lit, the fire's been started and the house is starting to burn.

A version of this article originally appeared in POETRY IN AMERICA, Poets & Writers Magazine *Special Issue, April 1999. Excerpts were from Charles Bukowski's "the Rape of the Holy Mother,"* Septuagenarian Stew: Stories & Poems *(Black Sparrow Press, 1990).*

—*Guy LeCharles Gonzalez*

Bios

Roger Bonair-Agard is the 1999 National Slam Individual Champion and author of *...and chaos congealed*, a collection of poems from Fly by Night Press.

Stephen Colman, a teacher and an activist, is the grammar poet on the PBS adult literacy program *TV411* and was named the 1999 Nuyorican Poets Cafe Fresh Poet of The Year.

Guy LeCharles Gonzalez, founder of NYC's acclaimed *a little bit louder* reading series, "attacks performance poetry with a perfectionist's zeal that pays off with a savage, cutting presence and a breadth of subjects..." according to Victor D. Infante in the *OC Weekly*.

Alix Lindsey Olson is a 1999 New York Foundation for the Arts Fellow and believes the world and poetry can change each other. Her first book is entitled *Only the Starving Favor Peace*.

Lynne Procope is a Trinidadian woman poet who is learning new things every day.

Left to Right: Guy Lecharles Gonzalez, Roger Bonair-Agard, Alix Lindsey Olson, Stephen Colman, & Lynne Procope

Acknowledgements

Guy LeCharles Gonzalez thanks his wife, Salome, first and foremost. Without you, this means nothing. Much love and respect to my teamates - Lynne, Alix, Steve and Roger for giving me the confidence that I needed to get through it all. Special thanks to everyone that made the Cafe a special place that year - Dot, Sabrina, LaVerne, The Goods,and everyone that saw through the device and made it worth the hassle. Extra special thanks to Marty, Peter, Eric, Stacyeann,Omar, Seve, and everyone else who has stepped through the doors of 13 Bar Lounge and helped to establish a new home.

Alix Olson thanks: Mom, Dad, Kathy, Liz, and George for being a family that has faithfully loved and nurtured my brain and passion; Jill, Sarah, Natalia, Liz, Sam, and David, my chosen family, for holding my hand and for caring about the world so damn much; Keith Roach for giving me a beginning in this weird art; Roger, Lynne, Steve, and Guy for being brave and honest cultural workers; and Amy Neevel, my love and co-thinker, for everything.

Lynne Procope says thank you Mummy and Daddy for the first book you bought me and the way you tell everyone that i'm a Poet. To my grandmother Beryl; i love and miss you and wish that you could touch this book, thank you for expecting only the best from me. ...I should pause here and say a word of thanks for the gift of the institution that is the Nuyorican Poets Cafe, an amazing home for the spoken word, which i hope will survive all. To the *louder crew*, i love you all and i can't imagine life or my craft without you. To Coach Rog, Guy, Steve and Alix thanks for making me memorize those damn poems and for being an inspiring and constant presence in my life.

Roger Bonair Agard would like to thank: "my team: Alix, Guy, Lynne, Steven for their hard work, trust and belief in me as coach even when I didn't believe in me. Their talents afforded me an excellent opportunity and undeserved accolades. I would also like to thank the Nuyorican Poets Café and Keith Roach for having put me in a position to work with writers who can potentially impact all canon.

Steve Colman would like to thank his mother for being a great friend and example, for encouraging inciteful writing, and for generously sharing her resources. Her wit, integrity, passion, commitment to telling women's stories, and fierce public speaking persona continue to inspire his life and art. He would like to thank his talent-for-milleniums-singer-songwriter brother Jon and his take-over-the-world sister-in-law Katrin for sharing their home and humor, and his weaving-the-word father for sharing for all those weekly spoken word performances. He would like to thank his outstanding historian brother David, who through his brilliant critiques, enthusiastic support, sharp analysis, ear for rhythm, and commitment to revolution, is a co-writer of his life and poetry. He would like to thank another outstanding historian, Crystal for her smile and cheers and for challenging him in all the right ways. He would also like to thank the entire New York/New Jersey poetry community, his slam teammates, and Sarah Jones, mums the Schemer, Felice Belle, Keith Roach, Miguel Algarin, Lois Griffith, and the Nuyorican Poet' Cafe for providing the world with a space that has nurtured so many talented poets. The Cafe is a treasure...a living room of our own.